THE JUICE IS IN THE JOURNEY

THE JUICE IS IN THE JOURNEY

A Southern Girl's Travels through Social Injustice and Spiritual Evolution

SUE PRITCHETT

LIGHTNING PRESS LTD.
Black Mountain, NC

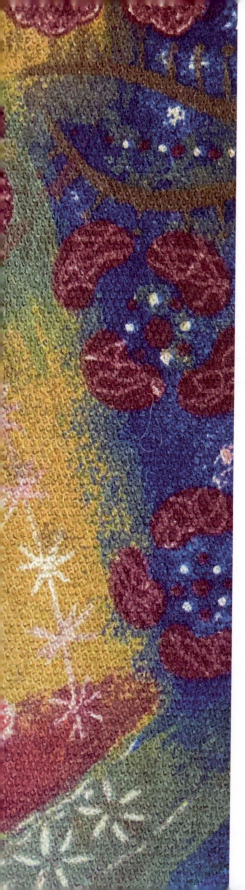

Copyright © 2023 by Sue Pritchett.

Photographs on pages 13, 28, 30, 39, 50, 52, 53, 89, 91, 92, 95, 96, 99 and 106 by Sue Pritchett

Design and illustration by Odette Colón

All rights reserved. This book or any portion thereof may not be reproduced or used in any manner whatsoever without the express written permission of the publisher except for the use of brief quotations in a book review.

If you would like to order more copies of *The Juice is in the Journey,* go to Lulu.com and search under the book title for the author's name.

Lightening Press Ltd.

Black Mountain, NC

Print ISBN: 978-1-304-90694-6

Imprint: Lulu.com

Printed in the United States of America.

TO MARY

If not for her, this book would likely be lounging on the procrastination shelf. She lovingly helped convert my babble into organized, readable text, contributed to the project in many ways and is my biggest fan.

PROLOGUE
The Freshly Plowed Earth of My Childhood

Walking behind the plow, I would feel giddy from the aroma of an earthy mix of smells and the thrill of being in the field with my father and my beloved mule Pete—who I was sure would give me a ride home on his enormous back when the plowing was done.

The dark earth being turned was soft and warm to my small bare feet. My 5-year-old body stretched in an attempt to step into my father's footprints. It was so quiet you could hear the buzzing of insects and the swish of Pete's tail as he swatted them away. My father's occasional gentle "gee" or "haw" to direct Pete down the long rows would barely break the silence in my sun-drenched world.

The rich, bold smell of the soil would be enough, but when mixed with the sweat from Pete and my father—plus the lingering fragrance of an occasional animal fart—it was an exquisite creation that would hang in the back of my throat for a lifetime.

INTRODUCTION

I was a curious and sensitive child. Born deep in the pines of rural Georgia during the Great Depression, and now delighted by the gender-bending 2020s at the ripe age of 90, I sometimes wonder how I stumbled into what some folks might call historical moments. This life journey is juicy, y'all, and I can say that the injustices I witnessed as a skinny Southern white kid stirred me up for a lifetime. So I set out to change a few little things. Honestly, any successes along the way can be attributed mostly to the fact that I didn't know any better. My ideas seemed to emerge from either my gut or my heart.

I pondered the urging of both my own inner elder as well as the advice of dear friends to get these stories down on paper while I still can. I kept thinking: Who would even care to read about racial awareness rising in my heart during Jim Crow? About birthing a radical idea of everyday people taking charge of their own health journeys through user-friendly patient education materials back in the pre-dawn era of managed healthcare? Or about my sexual and spiritual awakening with Mary, the love of my life, in my sixth decade? Then, there was the youngest woman in my writing group, who cried as I read a rough draft of how I found myself joining a civil rights protest long before I knew it was a movement. She loudly proclaimed: "People my age don't know this part of history, and we need to know this stuff!"

I thought OK, maybe so. Maybe my lifelong inclination to think outside the box, to plow ahead and ask, "Why not?" might actually help someone on their own journey. And, while keeping your eye on the prize (thank you, Julian Bond) is often crucial to success, never doubt: the juice is in the journey. My hope is that you, the reader, might find a little pearl that nurtures your own personal and spiritual evolution in these stories. If not, well, these pages will make good compost for your tomato plants.

1

EARLIEST MEMORIES

I think I must have loved the womb. I was still lounging there two weeks after my scheduled birth date. Apparently I was very comfortable in that cozy, soft, silky space and in no hurry to leave. This might tell you something about how I move through life. I am a chronic procrastinator.

My parents were probably spending a leisurely afternoon (no doubt a Sunday) walking around the farm, then stretched out on the sun-warmed, soft grass in our front yard. It must have been late November since I entered this world on December 28th, 1933.

I was aware of a shadow moving over me that, in retrospect, must have been a large hand. As I imagine it now, I assume my mom was lying on her back and my father was resting beside her, leaning on an elbow and moving his hand around her belly to feel my movement. I am also very sure that there was a lot of love energy surrounding the three of us. My whole life experience supports this theory. We were a close, loving, playful family despite many challenges along the way.

Ours was a pretty typical, multi-generational farm family for that period in southwest Georgia. My family consisted of my father (Harvey), my mother (Mary), older brother (Harold), me, and younger sister (Jane). In addition, there was my maternal grandmother (Exa, aka "Gramma"), and paternal grandfather (John Thomas, aka "Pap").

We lived in a four-bedroom farmhouse that was built in 1845 by my paternal great-grandfather, Gideon. There were approximately 600 acres of beautiful undeveloped farmland, complete with a creek, hardwood and pine trees.

My father purchased the farm from my grandfather in 1915. He grew cotton, peanuts, and corn, and raised pigs, chickens and cows. We had a large garden that provided us with an abundance of vegetables almost year-round. As a child, it always felt magical, and I was eager to explore it.

The original farmhouse was built with hand-hewn logs cut from trees that grew on the property. Later, the exterior logs were covered by lap-board siding. The kitchen was detached—typical in those days, because of the high risk of fire. True to form, the kitchen did burn down before my birth. A new one was built and incorporated into the main structure of the farmhouse and the existing chimney, and a new dining room was added.

I have many cherished memories related to that kitchen. We frequently churned milk produced by sweet Daisy, our cow, to make butter. Many vegetables were canned in our kitchen, and peas and beans were shelled there, as well as under the shade of the pecan trees in our back yard. After school, we could hardly wait to get home because our cook, Lily, would often treat us to delicious, warm butter-rolls filled with cinnamon and sugar. I can still remember the mouth-watering aroma as she took them out of the oven.

When our field hands were working in the crops, they would gather around the large pine table in the center of the kitchen to have the dinner that Lily prepared in the middle of the day. There was usually a fight and scramble between my siblings and me for permission to ring the large bell that called everyone to dinner. It was very loud and could be heard from all of the fields around the farm. We would often run down the path to greet the workers and chat with them as they approached the house.

One of my favorite features of our house was the huge stone fireplace. It had a double-sided hearth between the kitchen and dining room—which I thought was magical—and it was a main source of heat that provided us with great warmth during the winter months. In the kitchen, the surface of one particular fireplace stone was scooped out, smooth and worn after decades of knife honing by my family and our cook.

There were also fireplaces in the two main bedrooms but they were not used unless it was VERY cold. During the coldest winter nights, my father would warm two blankets and wrap my sister and me in them, then carry each of us to our shared bed and tuck us in under thick quilts that were piled on top. That made us giggle and feel his love. Also, when it was very cold, he would rise very early in the morning to build fires in all of the fireplaces before we woke up.

In addition to our house, the farm also had two wood-framed houses where sharecroppers lived, and a third cabin constructed of logs that housed our beloved Lily. Lily cooked, helped take care of me and my siblings and did general housekeeping. Although we lived in the middle of nowhere, there were plenty of kids and animals to play with. I felt loved by my parents and all the people who lived and worked on our farm, some of whom you will meet in this memoir. As I grew, however, I began to notice a few dark clouds hanging over all of us.

I was born during the Great Depression and money was scarce for essential items we did not grow, but luckily, we always had plenty to eat because of our garden. During this time, the destructive boll weevil appeared in the South. This plague seemed to suck the life out of our beautiful farm, destroying most of our cotton, which was our main source of income.

I could feel the sadness and frustration of my father, see the fear and dread on my mother's face, and I could sense unrest among the workers as well. I was too young to understand what was happening at the time, but I felt it, and it frightened me.

We often had a hurtful shortage of cash, but I never remember thinking we were "poor." We survived the hard times with a certain degree of grace and love for each other, and never lost the belief that we could accomplish whatever we set out to do.

FAMILY PROFILES

Father Playful, jokester, life of the party, affectionate with a sad center

Mother Smart, creative, energetic, moody and witty

Brother Happy trickster, very handsome, girls loved him as much as he loved himself

Sister Good student, giggly, sensitive and cute

Me My family said I didn't give a flip and was "devil may care." I said they were wrong and I'm still working on it

Me as a toddler.

Harold, Jane and me.

Mother, father, Jane and me. My brother Harold is hiding.

A painting by my sister, Jane, of the farmhouse we grew up in, built in 1845 by my paternal great-grandfather, Gideon. It is still standing.

A side view of the farmhouse.

2

PETE

Pete the mule was a gentle giant and a "stable" presence in my young life; he was steady, slow and trustworthy. My 6-foot-tall father had to stretch to put me, as a toddler, on Pete's back for a little ride. Pete always stood very still until my father gave him direction. His kind, liquid eyes had a look of total contentment. He seemed to enjoy having children sink into his thick brown coat, hang on to his mane, and giggle with delight.

During the warmth of spring, Dad would find a shady spot under one of the many large oak trees and clip Pete's entire coat to prepare him for the long, hot, south Georgia summer. It was hard to tell who enjoyed this process more. It seemed to be a love fest between man and beast, with Dad patting, rubbing and speaking softly while Pete nuzzled and nickered back. Pete seemed to have a skip in his step on the way back to the barn.

My father loved entertaining children and would sometimes hitch Pete to a large handmade sled that was used to haul supplies to the fields, and we kids would be taken for a ride. This often included a trip to the store for a Popsicle a half-mile away on the dusty dirt road by our farm. We quickly learned to speak Pete's language, which consisted of: Gee (turn right), Haw (turn left), Whoa (stop) and Giddy-Up (go). Pete took his responsibility seriously to bring us home safely and no one ever worried about him becoming too excited. His only gait was "slow."

My brother Harold and me on sweet Pete.

3

PAP

I have many endearing memories of my grandfather, John Pritchett, who lived with us and who we called "Pap." He was already an old man when I was a child. A vivid memory is Pap sitting quietly in a green rocking chair on the front porch of our farmhouse and twiddling his thumbs. He did not talk much, perhaps because he was close to what we called "stone deaf," making communication very difficult. There were no hearing devices at the time. He also had limited eyesight and could only read the large print (headlines) in the newspaper. The Sears Roebuck catalog sold eyeglasses and had an eye chart to help you find the right magnification. He ordered a pair of glasses that actually helped quite a bit. However, looking back, even with us shouting messages at him, Pap's world seemed to shrink.

Pap was both feisty and caring. I found it amusing that, in his later years, it took the effort of both my father and brother to wrangle him into having his weekly bath and shave. Even though his balance was not the best, my mother said he would put his finger out for me to hold and toddle around the house with me daily when I was first learning to walk. When I was 5, I stepped on a rusty nail and Pap insisted that he would be responsible for my treatment. He cut material from a wool hat, set it on fire until it began to smoke, extinguished it, and had me hold my foot over the smoke. He claimed that the smoky oil from the wool would prevent infection, and it worked!

Pap never displayed much emotion, but I remember him revealing a level of tenderness that I had never seen before when Rex, our wonderful and cherished Collie, died. After my siblings and I cried our eyes out and our parents shed a few tears as well, Pap gathered up this beloved member of our family and took him into the woods to bury him. Even as a child, I was aware of the pain in his face and the deep silence that hung in the air as he slowly walked toward the woods with Rex. My father dug a hole and Rex was put to rest under a large oak tree. The whole family worked and cried together while creating a marker for his grave. I still carry that loving memory in my heart.

When I was around 10, Pap taught me how to "whittle." Using pieces of an old cedar tree that had fallen in a storm, he showed me how to safely use his knife to make simple shapes and images from the soft wood. Before long, I was actually making things! First, I carved little logs and made them into a small cabin about five inches tall - complete with a removable roof so I could create smoke coming out of the chimney. Then, when I learned how to carve a chain with moving links, I promptly and proudly declared myself an "artist". Every piece of soap in the house became a fish or frog; I even remember carving an image of my pet dog from a chalk block. And that passion has now lasted for almost 90 years as I continue to sculpt in wood, clay, and stone.

I guess this is my favorite funny story about frisky old Pap: At age 98, Pap walked with a cane and seemed pretty slow and unsteady. Our barn was about two blocks from the farmhouse porch. Hay was stored in the attic and the bales would be tossed into a hanger just above a long trough so that the horses and mules could reach it. Pap enjoyed feeding the animals, and many afternoons he would lift his cane from the porch banister and shuffle down to the barn. There, he would hang his cane over a fence and climb up the very steep, ladder-like stairs into the attic. He would then throw down several 40-pound bales of hay for the animals, then descend the steps and walk back to the green rocker on the porch—without his cane. Later, when Pap was called to supper, he would notice that his cane was missing and be unable to walk to the dining room until one of us went to the barn to retrieve it!

This gentle soul that we called Pap quietly died of heart failure two months before his 100th birthday. One of my significant memories about his death was that just prior to taking his last breath, Pap smiled, held out his arms and said, "Oh look! Here comes Martha and Mary (his deceased sisters) through the flowers!" I remember feeling happy that Pap had such a joyous experience as he died. As was the custom in those days, Pap's body was prepared at the local funeral home and he, in his casket, was placed in the parlor of our house for visitation prior to his funeral and burial.

"Thanks for helping me learn to walk, Pap, and for teaching me to carve. I loved you even when you were ornery."

Pap in the front yard with the barns in the background.

4

TORRID LOVE AFFAIRS OF MY YOUTH

My first love affair occurred in the first grade with a boy named Jack. With red hair and freckles, Jack stood out visually but he was very quiet. He lived on a farm near me and got on the school bus every morning, one stop before me. When the bus arrived at my house, I was already smiling and hoped I would be sitting with Jack. When I climbed into the bus, Jack would already be on the edge of his seat looking at me. He would slap the seat next to him and motion me back. I'd smile and sit down as the bus rolled on. We would glance at each other occasionally but usually not a word was spoken on the trip to school.

Since Jack's farm was close to mine, we would also see each other after school or on a weekend. He would saddle up two of his Shetland ponies and ride over to my house, bringing one for me. We would trot around the farms and sometimes go to the little general store for a grape Popsicle.

I do not remember how long this love affair lasted and I do not even remember it ending. But life went on.

My next serious love affair was with Walter, a city boy who would gaze at me during our 5th grade classes together. He was beautiful—tall, with dark bushy hair and dimples. He was also very athletic, and I always tried to get picked for his team during our recess games. Unlike Jack, Walter talked - A LOT. He was very popular and I knew I had competition.

Then one day it happened! Walter's father brought him to our farm for a visit. He hauled his bicycle out of his father's truck and we went for a ride down the dirt road in front of my house. I felt awkward and shy but tried to appear very casual. I had never been on a real date and I didn't know what to call this, but it was "something".

We rode down the dusty road past two or three houses and through a small stream that crossed the road and made a turn. Walter quickly pedaled into a small path off the road and stopped, so I followed him. He got off of his bike and came over to mine. "Do you want to kiss?" he said, smiling. "I guess so," I said as my face turned crimson. The gentle meeting of our lips was short but it was very sweet. I loved the taste and the warm feeling, which lingered for a very long time. We were quiet for a moment, then looked at each other and grinned as if breaking some big rule and loving it. We rode home in silence but I sat tall on my bike and knew that I was now a woman of the world.

5

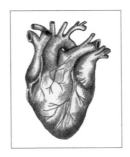

A FRAUDULENT ARTISTIC ADVENTURE

In my young years, artistic expression revolved around photography and carving. My most prized possession was my Brownie camera. I took pictures of EVERYTHING!—people, animals, dirt, rocks, EVERYTHING.

In about the 3rd or 4th grade, I discovered by accident (and a bit of fraud), that I also had a little drawing talent. A homework assignment for health class was to draw a heart. I found a picture of a heart in a book and traced it. When I presented it to the class, students said that I had cheated because it was too perfect. It was also obvious that the teacher was suspicious as well but she didn't say anything.

As the accusations piled up, I sweated it out and did not confess my crime. The teacher ended the discussion by inviting me up to the blackboard to draw a heart and settle the argument.

At that point, I quit breathing but told myself that I really could do this. As I stood up I thought that if I failed, I would be sent to prison or at least kicked out of school OR, even worse, the teacher would tell my parents and that would be the end of my world. The stakes were high and I COULD NOT FAIL!

The trip to the blackboard was very long, and every step rang loud in my ears. My body felt stiff and my fists were clenched. When I picked up the chalk, it almost broke in two as I held it in my tight little hand. I felt like I had a rock in my belly as I thought of being labeled a criminal for the rest of my life. Finally, my hand began to move and I watched a picture of a heart creep onto the blackboard, which was accepted by the students and teacher.

I could feel a hint of a smile on my face, but I tried to stay cool and calm and project a "Fine, so what did you expect?" attitude as I returned to my seat.

Although I knew that crime did not pay, and had heard that it was a sin to lie, for a moment I felt I had been rewarded big-time when my blackboard drawing was good enough to cover my deception. I was a happy criminal! This fraudulent deed was a well-kept secret, and is being included on these pages now only because my parents are no longer alive. The fear I experienced then has pretty much kept me on the straight-and-narrow since that time…well, sort of.

6

DISCOVERING LYDIA'S BILL OF SALE

When I was in high school, not long after my maternal grandmother died, I discovered a small, beautiful trunk of hers in the storage area of our farmhouse that contained a treasure trove of old letters, shopping lists, and deeds that dated back to the 1830's. I felt as if I had discovered a gold mine of family history and feverishly began exploring the contents. When I opened a very old faded, yellow document I discovered a bill of sale for the purchase of a young, slave girl named Lydia. "OH MY GOD! MY GREAT GRANDPARENTS WERE… SLAVE OWNERS??"

As my eyes peeled the words off the document, I felt a lurch in my stomach and the slow rise of hot bitterness that I wanted to regurgitate. Even as I write this, I feel a sharp ache flooding my heart.

What could I do? I was the great-granddaughter of Lydia's…owner. Could I share my feelings of disappointment and anger with my parents? Rage was not an emotion that could be expressed in my family, at least not openly.

I did have a solution for my "in the moment" anger if I was alone. I went to the back of our barn and found my anger stick and beat the living shit out of one of the walls until my hands were numb and the adrenaline settled. Then I went into the barn, collapsed in the pile of dried corn and thought about my great-grandfather going to the market, looking over the fresh "African merchandise," selecting a "fine-looking" young, 19-year-old girl named Lydia, paying $500 to the slave market and bringing her home as a piece of property.

The Bill of Sale contained the following words from the the Secretary of State's office, Charleston, SC, dated April 21, 1841:

"...and to take the Negro woman, Lydia, into his custody and possession and the same to hold and detain to his own use and behold, (as his own proper goods and chattels) from henceforth and forever, or the same to sell and to dispose of at will and pleasure, returning the overplus, if any should happen to be, after paying the said sum of five hundred dollars unto said executors, administrators, and assigns."

I tried to picture what that experience was like for Lydia, how frightened she must have been. I wondered what happened to her when she arrived at my family's home—How did they communicate? Were her family members left behind at the slave market? Did she ever see them again?

I also wondered how my family treated Lydia. Did they show her any kindness? Did they provide her with decent shelter and food? Were there other enslaved people on the farm who were allowed to comfort her and help her adjust? Today, I still ask myself the same questions. I was told by my grandmother that she thought the "slaves were treated "well" and with "respect" and that the family abided by the laws of the time. Of course, those laws were not helpful for the enslaved, only for their owners.

I was told that several enslaved persons remained as employees of my family after the 1863 Emancipation Proclamation. However, if they had chosen to move to the north where jobs were more available and laws more favorable, I didn't know how they could have paid their way. As a general practice, enslaved people were often given a stipend to buy essentials such as clothes and some food that was not grown locally, but these stipends were often in the form of "tokens" that could only be spent at the "company" or family store.

After discovering Lydia's bill of sale, I felt guilt, shame, and the need to beg forgiveness for all of my ancestors, my family and myself. But the reality of slavery was too big for apologies. It was something that could not be erased and would live within all of us.

I didn't realize at that time how the impact of that painful experience would shape my future. It propelled me forward into the civil rights movement, which was one of the most important periods of my life.

The document I discovered among my grandmother's papers, detailing the purchase of Lydia.

THE JUICE IS IN THE JOURNEY

7

SNAPSHOTS FROM GROWING UP IN THE JIM CROW SOUTH

The Emancipation Proclamation was passed in 1863, but celebration by the newly freed people was short-lived since the so-called Jim Crow laws were quickly put into place in the South. They were a group of state statutes that existed for 100 years following the end of the Civil War, and were designed to allow Whites to continue to control the lives and actions of Black people. They included preventing them from voting, holding certain jobs, getting an education and other opportunities. Segregation was strictly enforced in terms of where Blacks could eat, shop and congregate.

"Race relations in the south are complicated," was a phrase I often heard when I was growing up in the '40s and '50s from people who believed themselves to be open-minded and were trying to be honest about their experiences living in a segregated society. Some Whites believed they were not prejudiced, but also believed that they could justify unequal treatment of Blacks. They believed that their "science" proved that the intellectual capacity of Blacks was not as developed as that of Whites. Others said that they had always treated Blacks fairly and equally but did not choose to socialize with them.

Prejudice can be subtle and deeply ingrained so that we often don't recognize it in ourselves until a specific experience brings it to light. This seems to be a human condition by no means limited to racial issues, but includes social classes, religions, genders…the list goes on.

Growing up in a segregated community with the cultural rules that dictated how to interact with your world was daunting. In south Georgia where I grew up, people had few glimpses of how to behave in a larger world. As I began to mature and recognize the "bullshitness" of prejudice and segregation, I knew that I did not want to play that game. However, there was a big learning curve in trying to follow my natural instincts while navigating racial issues and rules.

As a sensitive child, I remember my confusion: first, for example, we couldn't sit at a table and eat together, but we could play together. As we grew older, we could no longer play together. I resented these rules and began to question them. I didn't think it was fair. It slowly dawned on me that the unwritten rules centered around one: "How could the color of one's skin make them 'bad'?" The sad truth was, with early childhood conditioning, I wasn't sure it was possible to totally erase the color line.

Why didn't I speak up when the White neighbor scoffed at my mother's lack of concern as I played with the Black kids who lived on our property?

Or, why didn't I ask Lily, our domestic worker and second mama, why we couldn't eat meals in our house together? It was, no doubt, due to the overarching rule of our culture that children never talked back to adults, no matter their race. The quashing of my desire to openly express my love to people I loved and who loved me, I'd venture to say, was the catalyst for my involvement in Civil Rights work.

After reaching adulthood, I firmly believed that skin color could not dictate who I liked, who I dated or married, or who I developed deep relationships with. But it was awkward. I often wondered:

Did I say the wrong thing?

Am I being authentic?

If I don't want to date him, will he blame race as the reason?

In the dark corners of my psyche, will I be unconsciously influenced by race?

Will I think it's cool to date black guys because I'm rebellious and want to make a statement?

Is he my friend or is he my "Black" friend? And does that mean he's my "token" Black friend?

Blacks often bonded with white families that they worked for and they cared deeply for the children they helped raise, even as they followed the segregated rules of conduct. Scenes from the 2011 movie "The Help" offer accurate examples of the powerless world Blacks had to navigate. They really had few options but to "stay in their place" where they had been assigned by Whites. It was literally a matter of life and death. Although laws have changed and injustice is not as blatant, we all know that we are still chasing that equal justice world.

It was my nature to want to fix things and to solve problems. I was often frustrated and felt helpless; there was so much that I didn't understand. Segregation made no sense to me

It was complicated.

Lily

Lily Perry was a tall, strong, brown-skinned woman who was friendly and had an easy smile which displayed a beautiful gold tooth. She was not shy and had a matter-of-fact manner of speech. "All of you chillun, get outta da house…I'm busy!" Lily worked for my parents and I can still see her walking up the path to our house wearing a colorful head scarf and carrying a load of freshly ironed clothes in a basket balanced on top of her head.

Lily was a no-nonsense mother to her children as well as to me and my siblings. We all played together and, if there was trouble, she disciplined us equally. She also told us the most wonderful stories. We loved her and knew that she loved us.

Lily lived in a small log cabin on my family's farm just a short walk from our house, and I loved going there with her. The front porch was shaded by large oak trees and always felt cool and inviting. Her kitchen had a pretty, white, wood-burning cook stove that often held an enticing pot of collard greens on top and an iron skillet of cornbread in the oven. I'd be overcome by the aroma and and would blurt out, "Lily, I'm hungry!" and she would laugh and reply, "Oh, Lordy, Chile, let's get you sump'n to eat!"

Lily was there for us day or night, but not because she feared losing her job. There was genuine respect between our families. When I was 3, my brother was in the hospital and my mother often stayed with him overnight. I had a hard time sleeping without mother's presence; if my father wasn't able to console me, he would call Lily, who would come and rock me to sleep. I can still hear her soft hum, and feel her warm, comforting bosom. When Lily was sick, my parents worried about her welfare, and Dad would take her for medical care and bring her hot soup from our house.

Crossing the color line with children our age was not so complicated. We were curious about some of our differences and felt free to explore them. Gabe, Lily's son, who was just a little older than us, would occasionally stay with us while our parents were out for the evening. We would make snacks and sit around the big dining room table (that we didn't realize was reserved for Whites,) and often laughed about things like how our hair was different, while feeling each other's hair and giggling.

One evening, my parents came home while we were all sitting around the table yukking it up and enjoying our sandwiches. They stood in the entryway, looked at us, then each other with an amused smile, hinting that a social taboo had been breached, but never said a word. While I think I was aware that the Black workers always ate at a different table, I did not connect the dots at that time.

Later, when Lily no longer worked for us but still lived on our property, she would often come to visit when I was home from college and surprise me with a favorite pie.

She always made the most scrumptious snacks and she would laugh at my outrageous enthusiasm. BUT, we never sat down at our table to enjoy that dessert together. It always irked me that it was fine for me to go to Lily's home to have a meal with her when I was a small child, but the rules were not the same at our house for Lily. She couldn't sit at our table and have a social conversation with my family. This was never verbalized in any way, it just "was!"

I have no doubt that my parents "loved" Lily, but they had no framework, no history or clue about racial equality. They lived by unspoken rules that were passed from their ancestors. And so did Lily.

It was complicated.

Lily's Collard Recipe

2 Bunches fresh collards well rinsed

2 slices bacon boiled in 2 cups water for 5-6 minutes

Remove and discard major stems from collards

Chop collards into 1-2 inch pieces and place in dutch oven or similar pot

Add 1 cup chicken broth

Pour the two cups of boiled water with bacon over the collards

Add: 1 TBL. Balsamic vinegar

1 TBL. Red wine vinegar

1 TBL. honey (more later if collards are bitter)

1 tsp. salt

6 dashes Tabasco or other hot sauce

Bring to boil, cover, turn down to low and simmer for one hour or more

(depending on taste and desired tenderness)

Liquid level should be approximately level with top of collards

(add more chicken broth or water if necessary)

If desired, saute 1/2 chopped onion in butter or oil

and add at the beginning of cooking time

Lily's Advice: "I changes it as I feel like."

The expression on Hassie's face tells the whole story: tired and resigned, yet, determined and hopeful.

How Would You Smell If This Was Your Life??!!

As a child, the most absurd and unkind remark I remember a White neighbor say to my mother was, "Mary, don't let your children play with those 'nigga' children. They are dumb, dirty, and they stink." I wanted to SCREAM, but I remembered the unspoken rule that children do not argue with either Black or White adults. My response lay silent and bitter in my gut until now, as I put on paper what I wanted to say:

"Do you know what is involved for a Black worker on our farm to take a bath??

Pretend that person is YOU, and you have been in the field all day under the blazing, humid south Georgia sun. You walk home hot, sweaty, exhausted and dirty. You speak to your children—the oldest has been watching the others—and everybody is hungry, hot and probably a little bit whiny. There is no time to sit down for a minute and catch your breath. Daylight's a-wasting and it's time to cook dinner and wash yourself and the kids. So…

1. You trudge out to the woodpile for wood and light a fire in the little potbellied stove in the kitchen.
2. You trudge back out to the well, draw water—two buckets at a time—haul them inside and put some on the stove to heat.
3. While the water heats, you spend a few minutes with the children and get ready to cook supper.
4. You haul the hot water into the other room where the beds share space with a metal tub, pour the water in, pull the curtain, and manage a quick bath to wash off your day.
5. After supper you help the kids with their homework and their baths, or maybe skip the baths altogether because everyone is just too tired.
6. The next day it begins all over again.

It was complicated.

Payday At The Farm

Payday was on Saturday morning, when the Black workers (some were day laborers, others sharecroppers) came for their wages. My Dad sat in a rocking chair on the front porch with a large gray-and-red hardback ledger in his lap, and the workers stood on the lawn. There were other chairs on the porch, but he did not invite them to sit there. They only came to the top of the steps when their

Workers picking cotton on our property.

names were called. It seemed impolite, but apparently, I never asked him about it.

While that seemed strange to me as a child, there seemed to be a genuine friendliness between the workers and my Dad, as if the rules and expectations between them were natural and unquestioned. I never heard my Dad speak harshly to anyone, Black or White. Yet there was this gaping separation that puzzled me even at a young age. I learned many of the rules of segregation, yet they never made sense to me.

It was complicated.

—Our crops were successful partly because of the Black people picking cotton, hoeing peanuts, and many other back-breaking chores all day but, not sharing equally in the success.

It was complicated.

—Blacks could die in wars defending our country, but if their bodies made it home, they could not be buried in many white cemeteries. In a few churches, including ours, a place was set aside for blacks.

It was complicated.

—When the school that I attended was consolidated with a school in another county, my old school could have become available for Black children, which was very badly needed. Instead, the building was boarded up and left to rot.

It was complicated and bullshit.

The absurdity of it all was sometimes more than I could bear. The feelings are still with me, especially as I attempt to write a memoir that brings so much history to mind. In 1964, the Civil Rights Act was passed, but in many regions, Jim Crow mentality is STILL sniffing at the heels of African Americans. Although our country has made significant gains, I am constantly saddened by this fact.

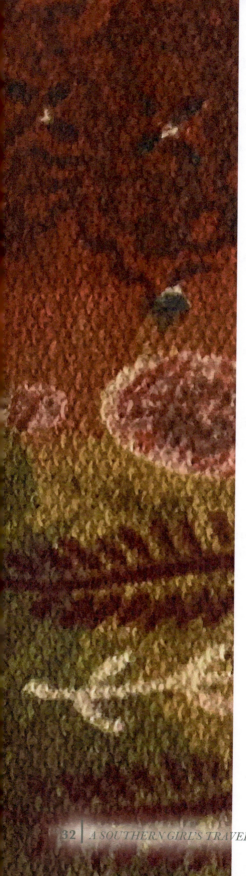

8

MY INTRODUCTION TO NON-VIOLENT DEMONSTRATIONS

The year was 1960. I was 27 years old and was spending a year-long apprenticeship in Duke University's Medical School Communication and Media Department. (See The Launching of an Unlikely Career, Chapter 12). The movie "Porgy and Bess" was playing in Chapel Hill, which was 20 minutes away. It was getting rave reviews and, although I was not aware of it, quite a bit of bad press from the Black community, which felt that it was promoting racial stereotypes. None of this was in our minds when my date and I and another couple decided to go to see this great musical.

When we arrived at the theater, we noticed from the parking lot that a line of mostly Black people was near the entrance, not obstructing the ticket office but close. My friends proceeded toward the entrance but something deep in my being stopped me in my tracks. I had to find out what the gathering was about.

I approached the line and asked why they were there. "This theater is playing 'Porgy and Bess,' a Black musical, and we are not allowed to go in," a young woman replied. "You mean not allowed to go in AT ALL?" I knew that seating in theaters was segregated, but…a TOTAL SHUTOUT? "That is ridiculous," I exclaimed. "Then I am not going in, either. I would rather join you!"

"Well," one of her companions replied, "We would love to have you join us, but you need to go to our college for an in-service about our philosophy, and if you agree, sign a pledge of nonviolence." "Of course," I said, and he told me where the meetings were held. My friends and I then went to a local bar and vented to each other about the situation before returning to Duke.

I had been involved in civil rights activities in Atlanta for a couple of years prior to going to Duke but never at the street level. Atlanta was trying to stay ahead of the violence and find ways to maintain peace, while trying to influence change that needed to happen. We usually met at each other's homes in what felt like a clandestine atmosphere. Tensions were high and our meetings usually included high profile Blacks and Whites.

Atlanta had a big head start with the Movement for several reasons:

—It had a very successful Black business community, segregated of course, but with good communication between the White and Black businesses;

— Three outstanding Black educational institutions were located there: Spelman, Morehouse and Clark Colleges;

—It was the home of Martin Luther King Jr.

Nevertheless, racist groups such as the KKK were becoming more active, which made us more cautious about how we travelled and in whose homes we met. Atlanta also had very high profile racist politicians like Lester Maddox, known for his threatening rhetoric. He liked to brag about the ax handles he kept inside his downtown Atlanta restaurant, Pickrick, if a Black person attempted to enter. Unfortunately, he was later rewarded by being elected governor of Georgia.

I went to the next local resistance orientation and signed their pledge for non-violent participation. The presenters were young, calm, friendly and very serious about how marchers were expected to behave. They also cautioned us about possible bodily harm.

I was nervous about being in the trenches, but I marched! We demonstrated in front of restaurants, government buildings, and other establishments that served the general public—except for Black people. We were screamed at, spit on, and had rocks thrown at us. Surprisingly, no one in my group was physically hurt beyond a few bruises.

I was amazed at the deep, calm resolve shown by my Black companions. It must have been contagious because it helped me relax a bit and match my behavior to theirs. In my previous work in Atlanta with the Movement, we were far enough away from potential violence that I did not have to totally conceal my anger and frustration. However, marching in the street, maybe just a few feet away from angry people in pickup trucks swinging weapons and threatening to kill us, I could see that the quickest way to get hurt was by acting out our anger.

My Black companions did not appear to be masking a seething rage and fear as I was, but they harbored something much deeper. They seemed to be calm to the core with no hint of a hostile interior. After a really scary incident during which I felt enraged and on the verge of violence myself, I mentioned this to one of my companions. He just smiled and said, "Aw, then you would be just like them and nobody wins." I took that to heart.

This was just one of the many "life" lessons I would learn over the next several years as I became more and more committed to the Civil Rights movement. Perhaps the most important lesson was that nonviolence not only confounds the opposition, but can also save your life.

9

RACIST WHITE BOYS ON THE PROWL

I was living in Atlanta in the early '60s and driving to Bluffton, Georgia, to visit my family. It was late afternoon and I decided to take a shortcut through a very rural area. It was curvy and swampy, but beautiful, and about a 30-minute drive from my parents' home.

The area was very lightly populated, and I passed what appeared to be a sharecropper's house. It was a small, old, unpainted clapboard-sided structure that needed some repairs. An older black couple was sitting on their front porch. I knew them slightly and knew the man was blind. They were beautiful. The man had a slight smile and the woman was also smiling, but with her head cocked in a certain way that made her look proud and independent and not afraid.

The sun was low in the sky, in that golden hour for prime photography. I always traveled with cameras because I was making my living as a photographer, and I HAD to stop. I told the couple who I was, chatted for a bit and then asked if I could take a picture of them. They said "yes" and I was in my bliss!

Toward the end of the photo session, a black, rattletrap pickup truck approached us that contained two scruffy-looking young White men. My history with the Civil Rights movement and my current location made me catch my breath as they pulled over and stopped. I had an intuitive sense that trouble had just arrived. My first thought was, "Oh my God, this could be really bad!" Unlike being in a group demonstration, I was completely alone. I was really afraid and began thinking up a story that I hoped would ease the situation.

"Well, look'a here!," the driver said to his passenger, "One of them nigger-lovin' WHITE girls from Atlanta in her little sports car. What in the hell is she up to?"

Looking straight at me, the other man said in a hostile voice, "What do you think you're doing down here?"

The sound of his voice rattled me and I was shaking. But, I smiled, took a couple of steps toward them and, with the strongest voice I could muster, said, "Hey, how are ya'll doing? Oh, I know these folks and just wanted to get a picture of them. I grew up here, my family lives near here and I've just come down to visit them. Ya'll live around here? I went to Edison High School; did ya'll go there?" They snickered a little, muttered something in a sinister tone and scratched off in their truck, leaving me in a cloud of dust.

I was really shaken but hoped I had seen the last of them. I couldn't help but be scared shitless that I would encounter them again. I chatted with the couple a little longer, packed up my equipment and left. "Oh, GOD, please don't let them be waiting for me around the corner!"

As I rounded the next curve, my heart almost stopped. They were parked beside the road near a swamp. I drove by them slowly and held my breath. "Damn, it's going to be a game!" I thought that my Triumph could outrun them but, with my knees shaking, I didn't trust myself driving on so many curves. I had many miles to go before I might see another human being and I was barely breathing. Somehow I was able to maintain a normal speed while they stayed practically on my rear bumper.

My mind was racing as I decided that if they stopped me, my story would include the fact that my father was the sheriff. Not true, but I was desperately trying to think of some names of powerful men in the area that they might know. I felt that I "knew" these boys. I grew up and went to school with "white boy bullies" who had a real mean streak. My hope was, that like most boys, they liked to scare people and act cocky, but were actually pretty harmless, especially if they were dealing with a 30-year-old white girl who might know somebody important. But I also knew there was the possibility that I could end up hurt or buried in the swamp.

I kept driving as they sped past me and then slowed down, forcing me to pass them several times. Finally, they dropped behind and I never saw them again. My shaking knees finally got me home and I don't remember exactly what I did to calm myself, but it probably involved alcohol. I didn't mention the incident to my parents because I knew how upset they would have been, and my father would have said something like, "You should know better than to be so conspicuous at a time like this. You were just asking for trouble". My mom probably would have sighed and worried about me for weeks.

I loved being with my family but felt baffled and kind of "undone" trying

The sweet couple from the infamous photo shoot.

to make sense of the many paradoxes of living in a social divide that was so complicated. I tried to sort through the love/hate/violence/passion all being played out among White people who I loved. I was saddened to witness that many Black people who I cared deeply about were treated badly and disrespectfully. It scrambled my emotions and made me feel crazy.

10

GUESS WHO'S COMING TO DINNER

In the spring of 1965, I was planning to dine in a very nice restaurant in Atlanta with two friends—one White, and one Black. Because of the racial unrest at the time, I made sure to confirm that Blacks were welcome when I made the reservation. My Black friend, who taught at a local university, was very shy and wanted nothing to do with public demonstrations. Even though all restaurants were, by law, integrated, I knew I would feel more secure if I spoke with someone there about it beforehand. I made a reservation and was assured that Blacks were welcome.

At the restaurant, we were greeted and seated in a very friendly manner. The wait staff was all Black and looked very distinguished in their almost formal attire. I recognized some of them from my days of working in Washington, DC, and riding the Southern Crescent overnight train, which was famous for it's fine dining car and elegant food and service.

As we began to browse our menu, a White male manager approached our table and firmly told us that they did not serve Blacks and that we must leave. I glanced at my Black friend and thought that she was about to turn white. I replied, "There must be some mistake. I called ahead to make sure that we would be welcomed and was assured that you did serve Blacks." The man said, "Well, Madam, I do not know who you talked to, but we are a private club; we do not serve Blacks and you will have to leave." "That is very odd," I said. "I have been eating here for years and I have never been a member of your club." My Black friend jumped to her feet, and I said to both friends, "Okay, I will meet you in the car. I cannot just let this go."

In a firm voice, I told the man that I would like to speak further with him and asked if he would like to go to his office or would he prefer to discuss the situation there in the dining room. The room became silent, and the watchful eyes of all the patrons and staff were on us. He quickly led me into a room off the main dining room.

After I introduced myself, he responded that he was the manager and began the "private club" spiel again as he shuffled impatiently and his face began turning red. "Please," I said, "I am aware of your 'private club' routine and you know as well as I that you are breaking the law. We had no intention of making a scene or causing a disturbance. We came here because I like the restaurant. But this kind of treatment is not acceptable, and could have been avoided if I had been told that you preferred not to serve Black people." "Well," he said, "whoever answered the phone did not know what they were saying." "Maybe not," I said, "but you have now set yourself up for a visit from the FBI."

As I walked back through the dining room to leave, every single member of the wait staff began hanging up their white jackets and walking out of the restaurant. Catching up with one of them, I said, "Please, I hate to see all of you lose your jobs over this. I did not come here to cause trouble." A tall, white-haired Black man smiled and said, "That's alright, Ma'am, we have been waiting for this moment!"

As I walked past the stunned patrons who had been abandoned in the middle of their dinners, I flippantly said, "Enjoy your meal!" That, of course, was inappropriate. The patrons did nothing to deserve having their dinner ruined. But, the "up yours" feeling I had toward the restaurant was irresistible.

Once outside, I shook hands with the tall man who told me they had been waiting for "this moment." Several other staff members smiled at me, as well. Suddenly I realized that the whole one-act play was brilliantly conceived and orchestrated by the wait staff and the person who took my reservation. They had been waiting for someone to show up with the right script to put the play in motion.

Back in the car, my friends and I quietly dealt with what had just happened. My Black friend was a little apologetic about her reticence to enter the resistance fray. We respected her position and, without asking a lot of questions, found another restaurant and had dinner without further incident.

The next day, I contacted the FBI, which had a special unit to deal with integration violations. An agent interviewed me, took my report, and then visited the restaurant. They later sent me a copy of their report, which indicated, that, in the future, the restaurant would be in compliance with the law. The unit requested that I advise them if I chose to dine at the restaurant again.

I was blindsided by the incident, but was becoming accustomed to unexpected situations. The civil rights movement was not a clear map or just a series of organized events. It involved people from different races and varied belief systems responding to life that was being played out in unpredictable ways in a highly charged environment. It felt electrifying at times and often dangerous. But, in the midst of the brutality and sadness, there was an almost overwhelming beauty and humility in the quiet determination that moved people toward their freedom.

11

A NIGHT WITH NINA SIMONE

It was a Saturday night in the fall of 1964 and I was living in Atlanta. Excitement was building throughout the city because Nina Simone, a popular and outspoken civil rights activist and entertainer, was in town. My date and I had tickets for her concert since she was one of our favorite performers.

However, our enthusiasm had a slight twinge of dis-ease around it. Actually, it felt more like danger if we gave it much consideration. Racial tensions were high in Atlanta at that time; Nina Simone was very open about her activism, and a touch of rage accented many of her songs. She had captured the tenor and heart of the civil rights movement like no other performer of the time.

When we arrived at the Civic Center, the air felt thick, the audience was relatively quiet, and appeared to be split equally between Blacks and Whites. The curtain was raised on the brightly lit stage which made the beautiful Steinway piano sparkle. A row of police officers marched into the room and stood side by side in front of the stage, facing the audience. The low hum of people's voices dropped into a complete silence of great anticipation.

We were seated in the center of the very large auditorium. I was excited, but felt a bit on edge as I scanned the room for the exit signs. I had already been in several demonstrations where the bodies were pressed together and tensions were high. I knew that we could find ourselves in the middle of a blood bath with the slightest provocation.

My date had a "deer-in-the-headlights" expression and I was nervously holding my breath. I was sure that some people considered leaving, but moving through the crowd and rushing for the door could have created the spark that would start a riot or stampede.

Finally, a tall, beautiful, strong, powerful, self-assured woman entered the stage. Her electrifying demeanor brought the audience to its feet, and several "Black Power" fists and welcoming shouts rose. Nina Simone was wearing a stunning red, sequined, low-cut gown and she briefly acknowledged the audience with a nod and smile as she strode toward the piano as if on a mission. She sat down, faced the audience and slowly surveyed the crowd. She gave another brief nod and then hit the keys, singing, "I Want a Little Sugar in my Bowl."

I was relieved that Simone did not begin the concert with one of her militant songs, like "Mississippi God Damn." The crowd settled and I felt myself begin to relax. Although there was a palpable charge in the room for the remainder of the concert, there was no eruption of violence.

Simone never voiced a single political opinion, as she was known to do. She performed a beautiful range of songs and ended with the emotional "I Wish I Knew How It Would Feel To Be Free," bringing the audience to its feet—and shivers down my spine. As we made an orderly exit, my date and I commented that we had been more anxious than we realized.

We visited our favorite bar and managed to change the anxiousness into giddiness. After questioning our decision to go in the first place, we agreed that we were glad we attended and SO appreciative that it went well, not only for our safety but to uphold Atlanta's reputation as a relatively peaceful city during those troubled times.

12

THE LAUNCHING OF AN UNLIKELY CAREER—
She Can't Do That... Can She?

In 1957, at age 24, I finally became interested in a career. I was searching for something beyond a job that just paid the rent and funded beach trips. I wanted something that required imagination, creativity, allowed me to use my artistic skills and actually contribute to the wellbeing of others. My great fortune was to work as an assistant and secretary to Dr. Walter Bloom, Medical Director of Intern and Residency Training and director of the Ferst Research Center at Piedmont Hospital in Atlanta, Georgia. Expecting another boring job, this is what happened:

To me, Walter Bloom had magical powers that seemed to change people's lives. Almost immediately, I noticed that I was not bored. In fact, I became more and more excited about going to work. I began to wonder, who IS this man? I noticed how he related to people around him. Students, interns, janitors, nurses, professors, administrators—all seemed to be equally important. When students or interns made a mistake, they were seldom reprimanded, but simply invited "back to the drawing board" for a joint problem-solving session. Dr. Bloom had a keen sense for potential. By treating students as if they had already realized their potential, in time they did. Perhaps that's what happened with me.

In addition to the usual secretarial duties, I assisted Dr. Bloom with preparing materials for lectures, developing film from research experiments and often helping with a patient exam. It seemed that I was learning new skills each day. Once he brought in a beautiful Leica camera and told me that the hospital needed a medical photographer and asked if I would take a photo of a very rare tumor. Since there was limited lighting inside the building, I placed the tumor on a poster board and took it to the parking lot to photograph. On another day he brought a drafting table and asked if I would prepare charts, graphs and illustrations for a publication. I hardly ever thought about the beach. This was fun!

I became fascinated with all the different education-related activities: teaching interns, residents, nursing students and patients. I also began to think about how much more effective and efficient these teaching situations could be with better teaching materials and techniques. I was hooked. Dr. Bloom's enthusiasm was contagious and I was catching it. In fact, I was on fire and began to actually envision a career for the first time!

Patient education really caught my interest and it did not require a PhD to observe that patients were not learning enough to manage their own care after discharge from the hospital. I learned that hospital re-admission rates were quite high, especially for patients with chronic diseases. Curious about what appeared to be a lack of formal patient education within the healthcare system, I began to search for more information.

Several research studies documented that patients with chronic diseases could successfully care for themselves with proper education, and that the reduction in hospital re-admissions more than paid for the cost of providing that education. The obvious success of these programs made me wonder why these practices had not become more commonplace! I couldn't find ANYONE who was coordinating hospital-wide patient education, and I was excited and energized by the possibilities of what could be created!

I had good communication skills, and was an adequate photographer and illustrator, but much more was needed than these basic skills. If what I was observing was common to hospitals and other health care facilities in general, a successful education model could become institutionalized and adapted to almost any healthcare setting. I eagerly began to consider where to begin.

I wondered how I could get grant funding to demonstrate the efficacy of these ideas and bring them into the mainstream. With only two years of college, I did not have the traditional credentials to apply for a grant. Fortunately, Dr. Bloom was an "out of the box" thinker, and more than happy to sign on as the co-director of the grant project and to be involved. He also advised and supported my efforts to prepare myself for this level of work.

With letters of recommendation and encouragement from Dr. Bloom, I secured an open-ended apprenticeship at Duke's Media and Communication Department in it's medical school to learn many of the skills that I would need. I was not formally enrolled in the university and the head of the department was not the least bit interested in "taking me to raise." He thought that apprenticeships were a thing of medieval times. However, after much persuasion, he finally reluctantly gave me a small work space and my informal—but extremely valuable—education began. It turned out to be perfect for my needs. After a year and a half, I returned to Atlanta with a document prepared by the Medical and Media department head (who by that time had become a good friend) describing my education and skill levels achieved…" just like in medieval times."

With space provided by Dr. Bloom in the Ferst Research Center, I supported myself doing freelance medical photography and illustration while I wrote grant proposals. My professional friends and colleagues with multiple post-graduate degrees tried to "save me from my naive self" by explaining that I could NEVER get a grant approved without a PhD or MD. Without even a college degree, I would be laughed out of town. I just kept my head down and continued writing, and to their amazement and mine, my first grant was awarded with all that I had asked for. Part of my excitement was the confirmation of my belief that academia was not the only way to learn.

During this project period I worked with several health care facilities in the Atlanta area and made considerable progress in helping hospitals and other healthcare agencies develop system-wide patient education programs. If we were successful, these teaching programs would become self-supporting through contractual arrangements with the agencies that utilized them. However, before the project ended, Richard Nixon was elected president in 1968, and in 1969 our funding was totally eliminated. I was angry and devastated. I felt that I was just beginning to hit my stride and had been excited about the work we were doing.

Now what? Back to freelance work while I tried once again to obtain funding?

There was a government effort in the planning stages to develop regional medical programs around the country to improve medical care. One of them, the Georgia Regional Medical Program (GRMP), was headquartered in Atlanta and organizers were interested in incorporating our patient education project into their program, which covered several southeastern states. The idea of covering several states was a bit daunting but, if that worked out, we could be back in business in a few months. We waited… and waited…

Meanwhile, my staff found other jobs and I began to pursue my options in the event the GRMP funding didn't materialize. SHAZAM!!! I received a phone call from Dr. Sidney Garfield from Oakland, CA, who wanted to develop a community health education program. He had heard of our work, was in town with a member of his staff, and wanted to visit. I had no idea who he was and told him I was very busy, but we could order sandwiches from the local deli and meet in my office for lunch. He agreed, and I showed them a couple of teaching programs and we chatted for awhile before they left.

I soon discovered that Garfield was a co-founder of the Kaiser Permanente health system, which became the first HMO in the country. I was impressed and felt

Dr. Bloom loved impromtu teaching moments, and so did the staff.

chagrined, hoping that he did not feel flipped off by my "too busy" attitude. A few days later, I received a call from him asking if I would be willing to come to California and consult with them about starting their local community health program.

What miraculous timing! I accepted his invitation, and in the fall of 1969 moved to California and spent almost a year working with them on their project. While there, they offered me a permanent position, which was very tempting. I loved living in the San Francisco area and had made many friends. But, I felt that my work in Atlanta was unfinished. I soon heard that the funding for GRMP went through and I was invited to join their staff when I returned to Atlanta. Again, perfect timing!

Over the next few years, we made some progress with hospitals around the region, but also ran into many obstacles. A new model of patient care was developing across the country called "managed healthcare." This meant more decisions were made by upper management, and direct patient care staff "in the trenches" had much less "say" about things like patient education. Top managers had a different mindset about budgets, and patient education support was often low on the list. It was difficult to make permanent advances. Even GRMP seemed to be moving patient education down on their priority list. Hmmm... Was it time to find another way in??

I seriously began to consider whether a free-standing patient education business could make it financially. Holy Shit! Can I pull this off? Can I support myself, pay the bills and still go to the beach? I had a revelation: This would be easier to achieve with NAN HULL!!! I had hired Nan the previous year to work with me at GRMP. Nan was not only a great writer and illustrator; she understood the human condition better than anyone I knew. She could communicate ideas and self-care plans to patients at all levels of education using simple language, illustrations and great humor.

YES! Nan was enthusiastic! We talked about the value of what we could offer and the satisfaction it would bring, as well as the financial risk of leaving our jobs and possibly becoming "bag ladies." We were excited about our ideas: We would start by offering consultations and workshops throughout the country, teaching health care professionals how to initiate and manage hospital-wide patient education. The objectives would include decreasing hospital readmissions and improving patient care outcomes. In addition, we would develop teaching materials that could be available nationwide.

This combination, if successful, would support us and a small staff. We decided the risks were worth it! We scraped up $500 each for attorney fees and "Pritchett and Hull" was incorporated in 1973. The baby was born!

A production room for patient teaching materials in the basement of Piedmont Hospital.

A staff development seminar.

13

A FLEDGLING COMPANY GROWS AND PROSPERS

Pritchett and Hull was a two-person, multi-tasking performance. Every morning while I dressed and had breakfast, my dog Tar (a black Schnauzer-Poodle mix) would press his nose against the front door screen. He was waiting for the roar of the ancient British Rover sports car which meant that Nan was about 5 minutes from arriving. They would enjoy a wiggly, wet greeting and then we would head to our respective work spaces—in my basement.

Nan and I rarely spoke except for collaboration on our ideas during lunch and our mid-afternoon break, which was usually accompanied by the sound of music outside and the laughter of children. My neighbor restored antique calliopes and went on a test run down the street every afternoon. Nan and I would get up from our drafting tables and march throughout our workspace to the music, twirling a drawing pen or whatever we had in our hands as batons. We would meet in the middle of the room, laugh, and then return to work.

The first 2-3 years were financially quite lean—as in living at the poverty level. Our days were delightful until the end of the month when we realized that bills were due and most of our clients had not paid us. This "slow-to-pay" routine seemed to be a chronic problem with universities, hospitals and other health agencies.

During these times, we would quit a little early in the afternoon for a "board meeting" to consider our current state of survival, which often included a discussion about which one of us would look for a paying job. The thought was so depressing that we ended up stretched out on the cushioned floor upstairs smoking a joint and listening to the good music of the '60s. That helped manage our anxiety and doubts, and usually a survival payment would arrive to carry us along.

Some people wondered what we were thinking, trying to start a business during an economic recession. Nan and I didn't know that we were in a recession, or even what that meant. I later realized that I succeeded at many things in my life because I "didn't know any better!"

We had, however, learned what patients and their families needed when they were sick, hospitalized, or trying to recover at home.

During the development of teaching materials, Nan and I worked directly with health professionals who treated and taught the patients, as well as with patients themselves. We made sure that we covered the information needed by both parties, and in a language the patient could understand. We were in competition with free materials that were produced by national organizations such as the American Heart Association, American Diabetes Association, and others. That did not concern us because we believed those products were ineffective for the population we needed to reach. Most of their's were not written in layperson's language, and were difficult to understand, especially for someone with a limited education.

Nan and I also planned and taught workshops, wrote and illustrated books, took orders for materials and carried out the packing and shipping. Eventually the infant

These two started a business?!

company began to show signs of growth and we were smiling!

As our business grew, the cash flow continued to be erratic. In 1974, Nan and I decided it was time for a line of credit from our bank to ease our discomfort about day-to-day operations. We approached the bank with confidence because of the long history we each had with this particular institution. Our banker, Joe, was very friendly and eager to work with us. We sent him personal financial statements, our business plan and financial data and he set up an appointment right away.

On the day of the appointment, we were ushered into a plush office and immediately joined by Joe and the bank manager. With very little small talk, the manager jumped right in with, "I have reviewed your documents with Joe and I'm very impressed with the P&H financial data and business model. When would it be convenient for your husbands to come in so we can take this discussion to the next level?"

Nan and I glanced at each other and I answered, "I don't have a husband and had no idea that would be a requirement—especially with my long history with this bank." Nan said, "And I have a husband, but he has no job at this time and I am the primary bread-winner. Does that count?"

"Well, ladies, I am sorry to hear that, but the bank's policy is that we can only approve this type of loan if husbands sign as co-borrowers. You understand, it's just a policy that most banks follow. As you probably know, credit card companies will only issue cards to a woman's husband or father." As we prepared to leave, I said, "I guess American Express made a mistake when they issued me a credit card 15 years ago." His response was "I am surprised at that, Miss Pritchett, but I hope you ladies will stick with us. We really appreciate your business."

Nan and I were angry and discouraged, but had to laugh at the irony, especially since she was much less of a financial risk than her husband. And, although I was single, I had a long and pristine history with that same bank.

A few years later, the bank called us to say that the rules had changed and they could now accommodate us with a line-of-credit loan or other financial needs.

PROGRESS? I suppose. I had begun to realize how naive I had been about discrimination against women in business. I began to pay more attention.

Pritchett and Hull quickly outgrew my basement and over the next few years we made several moves to larger spaces and acquired more staff, more equipment and more headaches. Nan and I had to decide who would be the "real manager" or CEO of the company. Neither of us was excited about the prospect, but Nan was more skilled in the area of writing and illustration, which was the heart of day-to-day production. I became the CEO and managed the finances, marketing, and organizational aspects of the business as well as continuing with consultations and teaching workshops.

The demand for our teaching workshops was increasing, and many of the professionals who were participants convinced their healthcare facilities to become some of our first customers. We soon realized that we needed more employees, more structure and a few policies in place. This would be fun: We knew we did not want to create a "cookie cutter" corporation. We wanted to have a working environment in which employees could earn a decent wage, learn new skills and be eager to contribute to the business in a way that benefitted everyone.

The first rule we made was that profits would be shared with employees. Our first obstacle was our CPA, who was quick to tell us, "Your pay schedule is above average and bonuses are not a good idea". We argued, "If the staff is responsible for the success of the company, why should they not share in that success?" Her reasoning was, "Because it sets a bad precedent in the industry and it is harmful for the employees. If they leave and try to find another job with equal or more pay, they will be disappointed." In other words, we should keep wages as low as possible and follow existing business principles with which we disagreed. We disregarded this "advice," followed our own beliefs, and broke several standard practices along the way. Here are some examples:

Time Off! We decided that every month should have one holiday and, if a month did not have a national holiday, we created our own. We declared that in addition to their annual vacations, we would also close the business between Christmas and New Year's Day, and staff would receive year-end bonuses based on annual profits. We believed that we should set our goals high, work hard, support each other, be playful when possible and enjoy a sense of humor.

Neither Nan nor I were really managers in the usual sense; we were both primarily right brained and, oddly enough, we intuitively hired people with the skills we needed. We told potential employees, "We are not den mothers. We hire people because we feel that they have great potential to contribute to the mission of the company. We expect people to learn their jobs, do their jobs, love their jobs, or leave their jobs and find a better fit."

We were a fledgling company and wanted everyone to make a contribution based on their special skills and ideas. Our loose organizational structure made it easy to shift responsibilities around to match the task with the talent. In all our years in the business, we were never disappointed with this approach and employees seemed to stay forever.

Rapidly changing technology made shifting and changing mandatory. One day, a staff person came to me to say, "We need a fax machine. Most institutions prefer to

◂ *Early Pritchett & Hull staff.*

fax their orders to us." My response was, "What is a fax machine?" I obviously was not keeping up with business practices, but said, "Well, buy us one. How much does it cost and do you know how to use it?" And so it went.

Computerization started with an outside company handling our database needs because at the time it required a room full of large computer electronics to accomplish the jobs. As computers became smaller we moved this activity in-house. Many of the drawing tables were moved to the attic since most of the tasks of creating a teaching manual could now be done by computers. Some staff had to retrain for certain tasks, but they were willing and enthusiastic.

Patient education workshops around the country continued, consultations increased and sales of patient teaching materials were beyond our belief! By the late 1980s, 85% of the hospitals in the US were our customers. We had sales in 30 foreign countries, and for fun, I must add that in 2003 one of our heart books made an appearance with Jack Nicholson in the movie "Something's Gotta Give."

At our peak, Pritchett and Hull had 25 employees. Nan and I never anticipated this level of response. We believed in the value of the business and had hoped that it would support us and continue for at least 10 or 15 years. We have both now retired and, as I write this in 2023, the business is celebrating its 50th year.

The success of the business has been gratifying. I loved my work! The greatest lesson for me over the years has been the demonstration that there are no standard rules or requirements for reaching our goals in life. While the traditional academic path may work for the majority of people, it doesn't necessarily work for everyone. There are many different routes to success. If the standardized path doesn't fit, it is possible to step outside the box and create a new approach. Creating my way around or through obstacles has often been where the juice of the journey has been. Although I enjoy painting and sculpture, I learned that my creative urge didn't have

to be that specific. I believe there is an artful approach to almost all professions—to all aspects of life. At its core, this is love of life. For this, I am very grateful.

A patient teaching workshop and early samples of Pritchett & Hull teaching manuals.

14

NEPENTHE, A PLACE OF NO SORROW

The year was 1977. My partner, Cynthia, and I were sitting in a restaurant near Big Sur, California. The name of the restaurant was Nepenthe and it sat at least 750 feet above the Pacific ocean—a breathtaking view. We took our time eating lunch and began discussing our trip back home to Monroe, Georgia, a very rural, small, conservative area just outside Atlanta.

There was little manufacturing in Monroe; farmers were having a hard time making a living and some small farms were succumbing to giant agricultural corporations. We pondered whether families could increase their income by setting some of their acreage aside for more diversified products, such as organic vegetables, berries and maybe Christmas trees using a pick-your-own approach to harvesting. We wondered if we dared to test our idea.

Neither of us had a degree related to any aspect of agriculture, but we both grew up on farms and hoped that we knew enough to pull this off. The other thing to ponder was whether we could work this closely together without killing each other. Cynthia was a fiery redhead with a short fuse and a generous heart and I loved her. But I was a real wuss when it came to dealing with conflict, which could just about be guaranteed. "Damn the torpedos!" became our battle cry. Maybe we will both learn something.

By the end of a very long lunch and a few glasses of wine, we had virtually bought a piece of farmland. We were set on proving that small acreage farms with the right crops could result in earning more money per acre for less labor, and either provide a decent living or at least supplement the income of a working family. We based our model on a family of four, with one adult having an outside job and the children making a real contribution.

A family working together to achieve big goals was an appealing image. We were hooked on giving this a try. Even though we were not a family of four and would no doubt have to hire some help, we thought we could create a similar situation and document honest, workable data that would help us determine if we were on the right track.

While dreaming of how we could demonstrate the feasibility of our project, we forgot something—our full-time jobs. I had a very time-consuming job at Pritchett and Hull, and Cynthia was director of a demanding state health program. What were we thinking?! Could we possibly do this in our spare time??

We returned home and waited several days for the magic of the trip to Yosemite National Park to wear off so we could check our sanity. When the magic remained, we assumed we must be of sound mind, and soon found and purchased a 60-acre parcel of land in Monroe. We called our new farm "Nepenthe," not as homage to the California restaurant, but because of its definition. "Nepenthe" is the Greek word for "a place of no sorrow," but it also likely referred to the name of a plant from which Greek women made tea to soothe soldiers coming home from war. The tea was said to put them in "a place of no sorrow." In hindsight, we could have used a few cups of this tea ourselves along the way.

At times, I was haunted by the question of being able to work with Cynthia on such a major project. But it was too late for questions. We were already the happy owners of a beautiful 60-acre parcel of land. So far, we both seemed to be on the same page with our plans.

We sold property we owned in Atlanta and began creating the new farmhouse right away. It was built by a very skilled but eccentric hippie carpenter and three "interesting" helpers: a handsome potter, a delightful attorney who had become disillusioned with his profession, and a recently fired university professor who made the mistake of falling in love with one of his students. I was relieved to discover that they also knew what to do with a hammer and at some point in their lives had learned carpentry skills.

We wanted to utilize as many passive solar building principles as possible and, with the help of our creative and committed "carpenters," we ended up with a beautiful farmhouse that surpassed our expectations. The main level was a large open area with a kitchen, living/dining room, bath and small office. The upstairs was an open loft with two bedrooms and a bath. An impressive wood-burning stove on the main level had a flue that extended up through the loft and heated the entire house. An adjustable skylight relieved excessive heat on the upper level.

We had hoped to use recycled building materials whenever possible and, to our delight, we happened upon an old dismantled hotel in a nearby town. We bought beautiful wide-plank heart pine flooring, as well as wall boards, doors, bathroom fixtures and other miscellaneous items, which excited the builders. The doors were from the hotel—complete with brass room numbers which we polished and kept in place. The sub-flooring from the hotel ended up in a diagonal pattern on the living room wall, and a beautiful etched-glass door accented the entrance from the foyer into the living area.

It was almost perfect, but not quite, of course. There were a few hot summer days that were too much for our passive solar system to handle. However, we were only a few feet away from a creek, and often enjoyed reading the Sunday paper while sitting in lawn chairs with our feet in the water. We were amused when my mother and a local woman who worked for us were dismayed by the rustic elements we employed, and frequently told us that "those old boards on the walls would look much better covered with sheetrock and some paint." And, "wouldn't it be lovely with some nice drapes over the windows!"

Planning for Crops

After research on which crops would best fit our goals and resources, the winners were Christmas trees, blueberries and an organic garden—plus a few chickens—to contribute to feeding the family.

We decided to start with Christmas trees, and set aside about 10 acres of pasture near the main road. Perfect! We both still had full-time jobs so planting was done on weekends with the help of several friends we recruited who thought it would be great fun.

Fortunately, exhausting days of planting were filled with humor. I mean, imagine half a dozen women, most of whom had never planted anything, trying to mark off planting rows, measure tree distances, use a tool called a "dibble" to make a slit in the soil at a special mark, then someone behind them putting a "slip" (baby tree) in the hole, and yet another person coming behind with another dibble to close the hole and stand the tree upright. Sounds simple? Maybe for real farmers, but for type A professional women, it was anything but. Of course, some of the dysfunction could have been attributed to lingering hangovers and differing opinions about the proper depth of a dibble hole among the instant "experts"—who'd never heard of a dibble until that day. "Sargent" Cynthia, of course, frequently dressed down the new recruits to keep them in line.

After a few weekends of planting, the task was complete and all agreed that the field was a beautiful sight, with several acres of little trees standing at attention. But the happy, exhausted women were hardly able to stand at all, and were ready to celebrate a job well done. Everyone staggered back to the farmhouse for a feast of grilled lamb and veggies, laughter, libation, and a vow to keep their "city jobs."

Our next farm project was developing a small one-acre pond. Since we had a lovely creek running through the property, it seemed the natural thing to do, not only for fishing but for irrigation of the future blueberries, which prefer a damp environment. A dock and a small boat were added to the pond. Wild geese made a stop there every morning at about 7:30, and if I was on my treadmill at about the same time, seeing them through my window would make my exercise more enjoyable.

Since we lived on a slight knoll, we noticed that from time to time it could get very breezy. During that first spring we created "Kite Day" and invited all of our city friends out for a day of kite flying, fishing, soft ball, pitching horse shoes and picnicking. One couple gifted us with a beautiful white goose who quickly took to the pond. Kite Day was so much fun that it became an annual event.

A few days after we were gifted with the goose, I noticed that our new goose seemed very lonely, so we decided to look for a companion. Serendipitously, we received a call from a neighbor who had a goose that had just lost its mate. The bereaved goose was attempting to interact with his reflection in a basement window and that told the owner he needed a companion.

When we arrived at our pond with the sad goose we noticed that our lonely goose was watching us from a distance. We carefully lifted the new goose from a crate and placed him into the water. The two looked at each other for about 30 seconds and then hurriedly swam toward each other with wings spread in flying mode and almost embraced. From that moment they were never more than a few feet apart. They seemed ecstatic about their situation and so were we!

Everything seemed to be going well. The trees were growing and we hired students from the local high school to keep the grass and weeds mowed between the rows. The teenagers seemed to enjoy working on the farm and we appreciated their energy and good nature. I was afraid they might think they were at boot camp with Cynthia in charge, but they quickly fell into the rhythm of the work and a very close relationship developed. It seemed that Cynthia had some kind of magic with these young people. In fact, this experience led to our setting up a small college scholarship fund for kids in high school who were interested in a career related to environmentally-friendly agricultural pursuits.

Time to Think About Planting Blueberries

We identified 5 level acres close to the pond and marked it off for planting blueberries. Cynthia and I had an easy time agreeing on five different varieties to satisfy different growing times, tastes and sizes, and our soil and climate. We laid out the five acres with approximately 6-foot spacing, planted the small bushes and put a thick layer of rotted sawdust around each plant. Setting up the irrigation system was tedious but very effective. The work of establishing the blueberries was labor-intensive but the end result of seeing these tender baby plants ready to grow and produce nutritious fruit was a real rush!

We had mixed feelings about the many deer that enjoyed our property. Luckily, blueberry bushes were not compatible with their digestive systems, so they wandered through them but never ate any part of them. On occasion, small wild turkeys would nibble a few berries around the bottom of the bushes, but we figured we had enough to share. We discovered that birds would swarm the bushes for the berries but only when they were overripe and beginning to ferment toward the end of the season. Some of the birds became quite drunk after snacking on the fermented berries, entertaining us with their loopy navigation.

After 3 years of growth, the time finally arrived to offer blueberries! We were excited! The sales operation was "pick your own" and sometimes a "pay on your own" honor system. The check-out area was very pleasantly located in the shade of a huge oak tree with a container of cool lemonade and a few chairs around for resting and chatting with customers, many of whom were friends from Atlanta. When we had to be away for a period of time, we set up a sign to explain how to pick, weigh and pay for the berries. Everyone was invited to explore and enjoy the farm while they were there.

The First Big Day of Christmas Tree Sales

Six years after buying the farm, the first day of cut-your-own Christmas trees sales finally arrived! It was Thanksgiving weekend. The trees had been given a light pruning several weeks before and speakers were mounted around the property for holiday music. A friend who owned several beautiful Percheron horses set up a wagon for hayrides around the farm property. Bailing equipment was in place to wrap and secure the trees on car tops. The sales shack was filled with wreaths, bows, Christmas tree skirts and had a smiling volunteer at the window. (Many of our friends rotated through that position, but we always knew when our good friend, Glory, had been at the helm of sales: The inventory disappeared and the coffers were full on those days because her enthusiasm could sell Saran-wrapped manure, if needed!)

I was in charge of the parking area and greeting people, and with the help of four enthusiastic volunteers made sure everyone had a saw, then sent them off to the fields to select their tree. Cynthia played general manager and tried to keep volunteers busy and happy while she helped people transport their trees to the sales area in our golf cart. We had also arranged for Humane Society volunteers to set up in a small shed adjacent to the parking area, where they offered chili, hotdogs, and hot cider for sale to support their animal rescue work.

The energy that first day felt electric and festive! It was a blue-sky day with just a little nip in the air for families searching for the "perfect" tree, and the music of Meinheim Steamroller or an Elvis Presley Christmas tune floated through the air. Children seemed in awe of their surroundings and were fascinated by the huge Percheron horses that took them on wagon trips around the farm. After securing Christmas trees to their vehicles, everyone seemed to enjoy lingering to explore the farm, take walks in the woods, watch the ducks in the pond or share a picnic lunch in the wide-open pasture areas. What an exciting time for all of us!

As the first day progressed, I was happily blown away to see our overflowing parking lot, and the large number of families enjoying their experience. We didn't know at the time that we were meeting people who would make this a family tradition and that we would watch their toddlers grow into teenagers. How gratifying it was to hear from visitors that we had created a festive holiday experience and that for some, it was the highlight of their Christmas season. An Atlanta customer tipped off a TV network about their "Nepenthe experience" and before we knew it, we had two local stations requesting to film the festivities in an attempt to get some holiday spirit into their evening news reports.

And so it was. The seasons went by. Nepenthe quickly became a cherished and well- known hub of activity. People were eager to volunteer their time to work in "the place of no sorrow." In addition to becoming a favorite spot to pick blueberries and cut Christmas trees, many friends continued to celebrate kite day, attend sweat lodge weekends, spiritual retreats, weddings, family gatherings, and star gazing away from city lights. But there was a problem…

The Fly in the Ointment

When navigating through a huge project, it's unusual not to bump into obstacles. One difficulty during the creation of Nepenthe was that although Cynthia and I cared deeply for each other and had similar values, our personality divide grew deeper. We shared an over-all appreciation for the project, but trying to work together was proving to be a real struggle. We disagreed and became exasperated with each other constantly. Planning together generally worked, but executing the plan was often a disaster. We realized that most of our arguments about the Nepenthe project reached a high pitch because neither of us knew exactly what we were doing and that we were "learning on the job."

These situations were too frequent and the altercations were very upsetting to me. In fact, I had a tendency to lose myself in personal relationships and allowed, or maybe even encouraged, my partner to take the dominant role. As I look back, I realize that as painful as it had been, I had learned how to better navigate a personal relationship.

Most importantly, I realized that our continuing to live together was not healthy for me, and deep in my heart I had known this for a long time. Why did it take me 12 years to admit it? Entering into such a lifetime commitment was important to me, and admitting failure was just more than I could handle at the time. Finally, in 1990, we both knew it was over and we went our separate ways. We continue to care about each other, have remained friends over the years and communicate frequently.

A Footnote About Nepenthe

Cynthia and I were both very satisfied with what we had created at Nepenthe and we were aware of the potential for further development by a future owner. From our personal experience and all of that potential in mind, we were convinced that Nepenthe could produce extra income that could greatly change the financial health of an average family.

The joy and scope of the project was much deeper than I had ever anticipated and there were many valuable life-lessons for me. It was very gratifying to be closely involved with the many people in the community who worked, volunteered and enjoyed every aspect of our farm. I discovered much about taking risks and overcoming obstacles and learned to appreciate the "juice" in this part of my journey. The relationship failure was a big disappointment and very painful, but I was very grateful for the emotional growth that I experienced which has served me well throughout my life.

The roadside sign at Nepenthe Farm advertising Christmas tree sales.

The farmhouse at Nepenthe.

Cynthia and me cutting a Christmas tree.

Above: a happy money exchange between friends, Glory and Bob. Left: Cynthia, wrapping Christmas presents.

Top photo: our beautiful goose couple. Bottom photo: the Percheron horses taking visiting children and adults on a tour of Nepenthe.

A rare snow at Nepenthe.

15

NAVIGATING THE COMPLEXITIES OF SEXUALITY

Since puberty, I have been aware of my sexual attraction to both men and women. As a teen, I had crushes on Rock Hudson AND Doris Day. As time went on, I became aware that my attraction to men was primarily physical, while my attraction to women held more emotional energy. This was awkward: Sex with men could lead to babies, and sex with women could lead to the dreaded label "queer." Where I grew up in south Georgia, if I was caught having sex with either gender, it would mean the end of my world.

The first time I felt a strong attraction to a woman, I thought I must be mentally ill and I scared myself into a total sexual void. "Pay more attention to the guys," I thought. However, I did not trust myself or contraception, and babies were even harder to hide than being "queer."

How to proceed? Becoming asexual simply was not in my DNA. I was also not concerned with morality. At the time, I believed that I was a good person and that God loved me. However, I could not even imagine navigating the consequences of my being pregnant or being labeled homosexual.

So, at the age of 17, attending Georgia Southwestern College was a mixed bag. I excelled in making friends, playing tennis, dancing, and editing yearbooks. But I failed miserably at getting good grades and dating. The guys seemed to like me as a friend, but not someone they were eager to date, which affected my self-esteem, made me feel awkward and unattractive. I had close male friends, but felt more comfortable with women, so I remained in a state of confusion about my sexuality.

After my sophomore year, having declared psychology as a major and encouraged by one of my professors, I took a summer job at a very exclusive private mental health institute in Hartford, Connecticut. The work experience was incredible, and my social life was fantastic. A men's college was nearby, and many students ate their lunch at the institute's cafeteria.

"Hmmmm; what is going on here?" I kept asking myself as I was approached almost daily by men who were friendly, polite, interesting, and very different from their southern counterparts. I began to have better self-esteem and even felt respected and more attractive. Dating became fun, and was perhaps part of the reason I decided not to return to the South right away. In fact, I started taking courses at a local co-ed college.

Steve approached me soon after I arrived in Hartford, and I recognized him as the handsome guy on the cover of a brochure about the institute. We soon started dating on a regular basis. He was quiet, reserved and a terrible dancer but had a great sense of humor and I felt sexually attracted to him. Despite only dating for 3 weeks, he asked me to go home with him to meet his parents. I felt as if I had stepped into a cold shower! It was obvious that I was not ready to be "serious," and I ended the relationship.

Bruce was flashy and full of himself—athletic, ruggedly handsome and he loved the outdoors. We had great times together but discovered that there was no serious spark for either of us. Our relationship gradually evolved into a warm friendship.

There were other men, and much validation for me that I was not as unattractive as I had thought. "What were those southern boys thinking...??"

After a year and a half, I moved back south to be closer to my family and to find a job that paid more. I settled in Atlanta, shared an apartment with a college classmate and took a secretarial job at a local medical school. My new job was appealing because it allowed me to utilize art and photography, and I was meeting many interesting people.

Before long, I was dating a medical student, Nate. He had a slight build, sandy brown hair, a quick sense of humor and was self-assured, warm and romantic. After just a few dates, he thought he was in love with me. I was attracted to him and we had good chemistry together, but I couldn't come close to having serious feelings, so we called things off. However, we kept getting back together and had an on-and-off relationship for several years. By the time he graduated from medical school, I thought I was totally in love with him.

But alas, our timing was not in sync. Nate's feelings were changing, and he finally broke it off for good. I was devastated, and for almost a year he was the first thing on my mind in the morning and the last thing before I went to sleep at night.

I dated several other men who seemed like good matches, but couldn't bring myself to fall in love with them. One in particular, Matt, was so perfect and loved me so much, I began to question my sanity and so did my friends.

The next several years were sketchy in terms of relationships. There were short affairs with men, but most of my attention was on my career, which had totally captured my imagination and most of my energy. During these years I was spending much of my time with women and aware that I was still also attracted to them sexually.

I pondered the difference between sex with a man versus a woman. Was I trying to prefer male sex because it was more socially acceptable? I don't think so. The only difference I could determine was the cultural attitude about it. I was turned on by the "maleness" of men. Their strength, their smell—there was just something about it— that was so satisfying. Sex with women was also very satisfying, but in a deeper, more intimate way. My general opinion about orgasms was that they were a great gift from the universe, no matter how you arrived there.

My longing for a permanent relationship was growing and it was becoming more obvious to me that my overall enjoyment and emotional satisfaction was greater with women. I really wanted to be "in love." It had not worked out with men, so I thought, "What the hell, pay attention and damn the gender thing."

Cynthia (whom I introduced in the previous chapter) worked in the healthcare field and one of her co-workers introduced us in the late 70's. She was very bright, and I loved her laugh and her spunky personality. We began to spend much of our time together and before long, we found ourselves in a committed relationship. Although a part of me knew it was a **BIG** mistake from the beginning, I tried to make it work—for 12 years. I knew the problem was not about gender or sex; we shared the same interests and values, but our personalities were just terribly mis-matched.

Cynthia and I created an adventurous life together and we deeply cared for each other, but we never had an easy agreement. She was frequently prone to "hissy fits" and I never had to deal with this level of conflict before. It was a difficult lesson for me to learn to take care of myself, but working with a good therapist helped me unravel the knots. It was hard for me to admit failure and difficult to extract myself from this relationship, but in 1989 we finally agreed that it was over.

I was in my 50s, and felt that I had spent my whole life trying to figure out this "sexuality thing" and I was weary. There were many other aspects of my life to be explored and enjoyed—and I did learn something!

Me in a candid moment.

16

FINDING MY TRUE LOVE

I met Mary at a friend's large birthday celebration in 1989, and she later told me that she felt an immediate attraction to me. As soon as she entered the room, I found her attractive and with a drop-dead smile. I kept watching her as she interacted with other guests, but we didn't have much conversation that evening. We didn't pursue each other for 2 years because a close friend told me that she was in a relationship, and I was in a depression.

When not at work, I was spending most of my time at Nepenthe drowning in my self-imposed misery after I broke up with Cynthia. The failure of that relationship seemed to bring to the surface every problematic aspect of my past. And although I thought Mary was amazing, I was wallowing too deeply in my misery to pay attention.

One day, mutual friends brought Mary to Nepenthe for lunch and a swim in the pool. The day was delightful, with easy laughter and conversation as we spent the afternoon together. My cats, Bobby and Nancy, must have felt the good vibes because they followed us as we walked together on a shady path through the woods. I noticed how excited I felt when Mary arrived and that I felt flushed by the time she left with our friends. Was I finally emerging from my deep well of sadness? Yes, I was!

For several weeks, Mary and I spoke frequently on the phone, and finally made a plan to go out together for a movie and dinner. I was excited but felt cautious and nervous. I was beginning to fall for her... what if she didn't feel the same?

I don't remember the movie, but I can't forget the electric current that I felt every time my arm brushed against Mary's. Afterwards, we went for dinner at a popular neighborhood restaurant, and our lengthy conversations were so intimate that we barely touched our meals. At my home, we continued our conversation over a bottle of fine red wine, and spent the rest of the evening together. I had difficulty breathing— I was THAT enamored with Mary. And she revealed that she felt the same about me. An enduring spell was cast that night!

Mary and I continued to date for many months in 1991 and became very close, sharing our pasts, our hopes, our dreams and our feelings. She had a daughter in college who I would soon meet. By this time, I had fallen in love with Mary and was really worried, "Would her daughter like me?" I was very nervous the first time we met because the stakes were high, but Jennifer was poised and friendly and we liked each other immediately.

What about the age difference? After all, I was 15 years older. How would this play out with friends and family? As it turned out, such questions seemed unimportant because of what was happening between Mary and me. It was obvious that we loved each other deeply and we began remodeling a house in Atlanta together to share.

It was interesting that I had no trouble sharing the news of our commitment with family and friends. Everything about it felt SO RIGHT that all the old doubts and fears of acceptance just melted away. Telling Jennifer and her long term boyfriend, Bill, was a little scary, but their response was, "We know already and wondered when you were going to tell us? We think it is great!"

That was in the fall of 1991. By then, I no longer felt any confusion or conflict about my sexuality. I am still attracted to both men and women and just enjoy the feelings. Real love is so complex and so much bigger than just sexual attraction. I also discovered that I did not have to lose any part of myself in a relationship, and that, in fact, with Mary I could become even more of my authentic self and thrive.

Signing for our marriage license.

After sharing 20 happy years together, same-sex marriage had become legal in a few states. We traveled to Newburyport, Massachusetts in 2011 and "got hitched," as Mary's father lovingly pronounced. We had envisioned the two of us tying the knot before a justice of the peace, but several dear friends got wind of our plan and had another vision. They created a beautiful, private venue on a friend's lovely patio for us to exchange our vows, and hired a caterer for a small celebratory wedding dinner afterwards. It was perfect!

Life is good and I will end this with a piece I wrote for Mary on her 71st birthday:

TO KNOW YOU BY HEART

To watch you when you sleep,
makes my heart feel warm.
To see you laugh when we play,
makes my heart jump for joy.

To see your look of concern when I am sad,
makes my heart feel loved and cared for.

To know you have even one sad moment,
makes my heart break and want to help.

To feel you when we make love,
makes my heart melt and
spread throughout my entire world.

To know you by heart is more than my heart
can comprehend, and sometimes
it thinks it might "bust."

MY HEART SAYS, "THANK YOU MARY, AND HAPPY BIRTHDAY!"

It really happened!

At a Community Garden celebration.

17

MYSTICAL YEARNINGS AND THE SEARCH FOR SPIRIT

My first experience with organized religion was attending a Primitive Baptist Church in the '40's with my parents which, fortunately, was only held once a month. The pews, very hard and in a horseshoe arrangement, seated male members on one side and female members on the opposite side. Families like mine, the "unsaved, non-members," sat in the middle and were the largest group.

The sermon consisted primarily of the preacher yelling at the congregation for an hour about what wretched, doomed sinners we were. He would start off with a calm, soothing voice, reading a little Scripture, usually from the Old Testament. Then, with a pause and maybe a bit of pacing around the pulpit, his voice would gradually build into a wild, spit-flying, Bible-pounding frenzy.

I wanted to hide under the pew but couldn't because my eyes were glued to the spectacle of what was surely a heart attack waiting to happen. I didn't dare look at one of my siblings at this time because a glimpse of each other's facial expressions could bring on a joint, uncontrollable burst of laughter. Mercifully, this tirade would eventually wind down to soft sputtering, sweat wiping, and a lot of breath-catching grunting. That was followed by the welcomed relief of a few songs in beautiful a cappella shape note singing by the congregation.

The service began by being greeted and kissed by friends, families and neighbors, and ended with us in an altered state with ringing ears. Not a very uplifting experience for my young mind and heart.

Although my parents believed in God and tried to follow a spiritual path, the only religious expressions were before our meals. No one in my immediate family was a member of a church, and my father was very clear on the subject, frequently saying, "I go to church for the fellowship but I will not tolerate any organized religion coming between me and my God." So THAT was THAT!

My only other exposure to organized religion as a child was to occasionally attend the Methodist or Missionary Baptist Church with one of my friends. These churches seemed a lot friendlier and certainly calmer. The preaching was still about sinning and burning in hell, but it didn't seem so imminent and certain. They even seemed to offer some preventive measures to avoid damnation. I had the impression that we might even be able to buy our way out of going down that path.

An awkward time for me at these services was at the end of the sermon, when people were invited to come and kneel at the altar and offer their hearts and souls to God. My friends would all eagerly hop up and go to the front of the church, which made my heart race. I wanted a relationship with God, but I was glued to my seat. I felt envious when they returned to our pew looking so saintly and happy, but I was conflicted between what I observed and what I felt internally.

The belief about original sin bothered me the most at that time. How could we commit sins in the womb? It seemed the only way to be saved from this original-sin state was to join the church, pay the dues and be "born again." It just did not add up for me.

By the time I graduated from high school in 1949, I had pretty much dismissed the possibility of finding what I was looking for in organized religion and was avoiding church as much as possible. One exception was the Saturday night that several restless seniors sneaked into the Methodist Church steeple where religious music was blasted out to the whole town every Sunday morning. On this particular night, we put our own music into the system and the next morning treated the town to Elvis Presley singing "I ain't nothing but a hound dog"— full volume!! Fortunately, the pranksters were never caught.

College, of course had many more distractions, but a spiritual longing still haunted me, and there were more options available to explore. Many religious and cultural backgrounds were represented by the student body. I went with several friends to various worship services and asked many questions. I discovered that my friends were much more interested in talking about their beliefs about dating, sex and alcohol than religion.

After completing college and moving to Atlanta, a big change began to take form. I was hanging out with a lot of Catholics, especially those in the social organization connected with the Cathedral of Christ the King. There were plenty of men and good parties, so yes, I joined the Catholic Church.

The Catholic bubble did not endure. I initially dove in hook, line and sinker, and actually involved myself in what I still consider "good works." As time passed, I began to notice what seemed like major contradictions between the dogma that was professed and the behaviors that were demonstrated. The generosity and loving kindness often seemed to be limited and have conditions. Phrases like "non-Catholic" were distasteful to me.

Universal love, but "for members only," did not make sense. What about my own mother not being able to receive communion if she attended Mass? What about my LGBTQ and divorced friends being banned from joining the the Church? Did the Church feel that it had a corner on the market to save us from original sin? Suddenly I was on my way to becoming what the Church referred to as a "fallen away Catholic"—another distasteful label.

Liberated from trying to make these square pegs fit the round hole in my soul, I once again tried to put dogma aside. I fell in line with my father's conclusion that it would have to be something between me and my God, spirit, or higher power, and I would just have to be on my own to discover the connection.

As time went on, I toured the metaphysical world, and attended conferences offered by the current gurus of the time in consciousness, psychology, and spirituality—Ram Das, The Dali Lama, Jean Houston, Marion Woodman, Virginia Satir—as well as workshops at Esalen Institute in Big Sur, California and an intensive regression therapy retreat with Barbara Findeisen in Geyserville, California. All of these efforts were beneficial, but I was still feeling unsettled and looking for something more.

In the-mid '90's, a friend suggested that I attend a meditation retreat in Minnesota that focused on spirituality and expanding consciousness. She knew I was gun-shy by this time and assured me this would be different and might be a match. She also persuaded Mary to join me because she thought we might choose to pursue this path together.

At the lovely retreat center, Koinonia, in South Haven, Minnesota, we were greeted by Barbara Cordts, the retreat leader and facilitator, a pleasant and attractive woman. About 20 participants gathered in a conference room strewn with pillows and chairs, and Barbara laid out a format that involved meditation and interactive teachings about the nature of consciousness. I liked what I heard, and even joined in with my questions. That was the beginning of a long and priceless relationship with Barbara, who wanted nothing to do with leading anyone down a particular path or running an organization.

On the contrary, Barbara's goal was to help us discover our own true essence and learn to live a more conscious and aware life; to transcend our everyday reality and experience a larger world view. The teachings dealt with the current human condition on a heart level that was life-changing.

We all brought neurotic baggage with us that would challenge any teacher. Fortunately, Barbara had a background in psychotherapy and could go into "shrink mode" when the circumstances called for it. In fact, she observed and commented that we were not only "fucked up," but a "spectacularly fucked up" group of individuals. We ranged in ages from 20s to 80s, and were males and females, married and single, straight and gay, musicians, artists, chefs, scientists, carpenters, teachers, physicians, body workers, healers, and more.

It was an exciting environment, to say the least, and sometimes difficult for me. The teachings often reached a high esoteric level and I struggled to understand. I saw that I had a lot of work to do if I followed this path and was not sure I was up to it. I often felt dumb and inadequate. But some inner knowing drew me to sign up for all of the retreats, dragging my guilt, resistance and frustrations with me.

Without being totally aware of when and how, my world began to change and enlarge. Neurotic patterns began to disappear or not have the same control. I realized that the "hole in my soul" had disappeared and my life was changing. For example:

- My sense of self had expanded and I was less identified with previous roles;

- I would fret less about small things;

- Days that always seemed packed with more than I could do were actually relaxed and everything got done with ease;

- My heart felt more open;

- I found myself listening more than talking;

- I was less dogmatic in my opinions about people and things;

- I felt less need to be "right;"

- I did not take myself as seriously as in the past;

- I had that happy feeling of being "in love" much of the time and felt more tuned into the world as well as the people close to me;

- While my desire was still to know more, I knew that everything I really needed was inside me—that I was what I had been looking for—even if I had not digested all that I am.

I have learned that problems are more easily solved from the inside out. When something happens in the outside world that is perplexing, I discovered going inside and listening to the knowledge and wisdom that is available through my higher self is a better path to a solution.

The pursuit of a spiritual path was and is no longer a series of dead-ends but an exciting journey of growth toward "becoming." Is my life perfect? No. Some of the old problem horses that were put out to pasture along the way show up every now and then, especially the one named "doubt" that hangs around a lot since I started writing. Usually, if I just acknowledge them, they are satisfied and leave me in relative peace.

   Over the years our group became a loving community which continues today. Although the formal retreats have ended, we often stay in touch in person and online, and support each other in many ways. The practice of meditation has been an important conduit to keep me in touch with a larger reality through which growth can continue.
I AM ETERNALLY GRATEFUL.

18

LEARNING TO FLY

I can fly a little, and even soar from time to time. I have experienced it in my body, my career, and my relationships. But, like any flight, it has not been without possible setbacks: stalled engines, becoming lost, and a few crashes.

Now, I seem to be just chugging along in a very old vintage conveyance with weak rudders. In the past, when ideas, excitement, or creative energy were bottled up or stuck, I was never without hope and belief that I would find my wings again. The fly in the ointment seems to be TIME itself. Age, and my preoccupation with the finiteness of life, floods me with an urgency to create and express a part of me that is totally blocked. I feel gravity bound and dumbed down. The will is there, the desire is there. I can feel the excitement but occasionally a cloud of insecurity creeps in.

I have always been a procrastinator, an 11th hour creature, but I never thought about the possibility of a scarcity of TIME. But what, really, has time got to do with it? I am still alive.

As I ponder this, I wonder: what can I learn from my past? In some of my earlier spiritual work, flying was often in my dreams and meditations, especially during retreats. Once, I was aloft in my own jet-powered "bucket" when a large spacecraft pulled beside me. It was full of my long-term meditation group companions and they tried to get me to come aboard. I thanked them but explained that I had to master my own current level of flying and would join them later.

Flying was also present in a recurring dream I had for many years about "feeding the masses." In these dreams, I was always responsible for feeding large groups. Once I flew a commercial jet pulling behind it an Asian food cart and managed to land it without spilling the food. Throngs of people were fed.

There were many other examples, mostly about teaching other people to fly small aircraft and picking up food for delivery to other places, much like a cosmic food truck. More recently I remember being in outer space outside my spacecraft without a space suit. I was taking directions from an aeronautical engineer about repairing a problem outside the spacecraft. After my initial fear faded, it was exhilarating to move around in the soft surroundings freely with no physical support.

Sometimes I wonder what I can learn from these flying dream experiences. As I write this, several possibilities come to mind metaphorically. In the small space bucket dream, I seem to be holding back—not ready for the big-time—maybe through fear or immaturity. When I was at the helm of the commercial airliner pulling the Asian food cart, I seem more confident but maybe a little reckless. Perhaps floating freely in space without physical support indicates some progress along a spiritual journey.

Maybe I just need to shed all the baggage, throw caution to the wind and enjoy the most creative time of my life!! OR, do I slip the bonds of this incarnation and just consider this lifetime training for the next one??????

BON VOYAGE!

19

GRACEFUL EXITS
My Mother Sets a High Bar

My hope is that we will be able to remove the taboo about discussing death and dying. Obviously, fear of death makes it a scary topic and many people tend to avoid the issue altogether. When family and friends refuse to discuss an impending death, it can make the actual event more traumatic. When we are removed from the process, we may miss the deep beauty and growth that can occur at these times.

When my mother was alive, we had many discussions about death—both hers and mine. Those conversations went something like this:

"Mother, do you believe it is a sin to take your own life?"

"Well," she replied, "I don't know about whether it is a sin. There are so many situations that can lead to taking your own life, like insanity or pain, for example. How could it be a sin in those situations? Some religions might see it that way. I have heard sermons that said, 'Only God giveth life, only God can take it away, and that taking your own life would be a sin against God.' I do not see it that way. I could never think of taking my own life, but I do not want to be kept alive by artificial means. Wouldn't that also be going against God? I do think I have the right to refuse treatment that would keep me alive a little longer if I believe it is my time to die. Who is to say that I am not in perfect harmony with God by the choices I make?"

"I agree with you, Mother, that we have the right to make choices about how and when we exit this life. If I have incurable cancer and am offered chemo treatments, I might choose treatment in hopes of prolonging my life to see the birth of a grandchild. Or, I may decide that I have had a good life and do not want to deal with drawn-out distress among family and friends. On the other hand, I may refuse treatment in favor of the

My mother's college photograph.

natural progression of the disease. If 'God is calling me home' and I allow artificial means to prolong my life, would that not 'go against God'? I might also choose to stop eating in order to not prolong the process." I do not believe that God would mind.

My mother sat quietly for a while and I asked her if she wanted to be cremated or buried. "Oh honey," she said, "people around here don't like to be cremated and I don't either." With a smile, she continued, "I want to be buried, but be sure I am dead before you lower me into the ground." We laughed and I said, "Don't you worry, Mother, we will install a bell right outside your grave with a string and you can ring if you wake up!" More laughter and we changed the subject.

My mother's wit was subtle but quick. She was playful, very creative and a joy to be around. She wanted to really LIVE every day of her life and when her time came, she set the bar pretty high.

When she was admitted to the hospital in November, 1990, at age 85, after living with congestive heart failure for quite awhile, we could tell that she intuitively knew it was very serious and that she might not survive. Her demeanor became a little more serious.

After the doctors did their examination and testing, they explained that they would like to put a stent into one of her major arteries near her heart to give it greater blood flow. Mother listened carefully as they explained the benefits and risks of the procedure.

She was very clear and replied: "Yes, I will go along with the stent. That sounds very reasonable, but please be guided by the fact that I do not plan to go home as an invalid. I do not want heroic efforts like artificial ventilation or resuscitation. If I will be unable to drive my car, walk to the post office and teach my tatting (lace making) class, then I do not wish to return home, period!"

The placement of the stent was successful, but the next few days were not encouraging. The morning after surgery, the physicians were having great difficulty controlling the blood loss from the groin cutdown site. Mother was very calm, alert and even enjoyed a little banter with the physicians and nursing staff. At one point, the doctor entered the room and began looking impatiently for something that he expected to be there. He called for a nurse, and my mother, hearing the conversation, said: "Doctor, it is right there in front of you by the window." He put his hands on his hips, turned to my mother and said "Mrs. Pritchett, do you want a job?" "How much does it pay?" she replied. You could feel the atmosphere lighten and it remained that way.

By the third post-op day, Mother's blood pressure was dropping dramatically and she did not look good. The doctor explained to me and my sister, Jane, that, "We are between a rock and a hard place: the stent is not working and she is losing blood. If we try to stop the blood loss she will likely have a stroke. There are a couple of other things we can try but the outcome is very uncertain. What do you think?"

Jane replied, "I think you should have this conversation with her. She is alert and totally capable of making decisions. We should all meet together." The physician agreed. He explained the situation and admitted that there was not much hope that they could meet her earlier wishes, but they could try. Mother asked several questions about what her alternatives were and listened carefully. Then she calmly replied, "I understand, and I appreciate your efforts but, no thanks." She made her choice fully cognizant of the outcome. She knew that she would not go home.

For the next three days, my mother was relatively comfortable and alert in the coronary care unit of the hospital. My siblings Jane, Harold and I were there. Many of our friends were also visiting "Mary" or "Mother Mary," as she was affectionately known to them.

Over the years she had become "family" to so many of my friends. I was always amused by the fact that when I was away on work assignments, my friends, even those with small children, would drive to south Georgia to spend the weekend with "Mother Mary." So it was not a surprise that she had a large extended family visiting in the hospital during her last days. The hospital staff was very attentive, made sure that she was comfortable and that we, her family, had a private waiting area with ongoing fresh coffee, tea and snacks.

My mother and I did not talk much about the fact that she was dying. There didn't seem to be anything unsaid or unfinished between us. Our relationship had always been close and easy. The only topic that we never discussed was my same-sex relationships. She treated everyone like family and never asked such questions. I never doubted my decision about this.

During her last days, I wanted to do little personal things for her that I knew she would enjoy. I would often go home, which was just blocks from the hospital, and cook something I knew she liked and bring it to her for dinner. She would tease me about my lack of skill in the kitchen. We had some light moments and she enjoyed visitors. Because she was close to death, the hospital allowed an unlimited number of people into her large private room as long as she was comfortable with it.

On her last afternoon she was still alert but quiet and seemed to turn inward. We sensed that she was starting her transition from this life. After a couple of hours, we said our goodbyes and she dropped into a coma. She died a few hours later with her loved ones at her bedside. The hospital allowed us to sit with her for awhile before calling the funeral home. I left her room feeling sad, yet full of love and gratitude for the gift of being with my mother during this deeply spiritual experience.

My wife Mary and I, having been together now for more than 30 years, talk about the end of life almost like we are talking about our next trip. Would the one left behind stay where we now live, choose a small condo with no maintenance, or would we need assisted living by that time? How would aging affect our decision? Just what living arrangement would we prefer? We talk about our real preference being that we would die together, but because of the difference in our ages, it's more likely that Mary will become a widow. We promise to try to stay in contact with each other and contemplate what it might be like in "the great beyond."

Occasionally, these conversations have a little sting and sadness, but we do not find shedding a few tears a bad thing. It just brings us closer and makes us appreciate the long journey we have had together, and the absolute delight we have found with each other. We have memories to laugh about and cry about.

We also both believe that true love never dies.

My witty, loving and energetic mother. She was "Mother Mary" to all my friends.

Mother's birthday celebration.

20

CAMPBELL COVE LAKE

The urge to create new things has never abated, but not because I chose to have a life of creativity. Maybe it was just in my DNA or I subconsciously followed a path that was already laid out for me by the universe. Opportunities just seem to appear and say, "How about this?" And I frequently said, "YES!"

In 1994, Mary and I quite accidentally discovered and then moved to a breathtakingly beautiful, quiet lake in eastern Tennessee. We designed and built a waterfront home that was at the base of Little Frog Mountain in the Cherokee National Forest. After living in chaotic, bustling Atlanta we felt like we had moved to paradise.

We designed our home to take advantage of both the lake and the mountain views, and had multiple outdoor seating spots to relax and enjoy the beauty of the area. It was a delight to slide our kayaks into the water in the early mornings and paddle with a thermos of hot coffee while quietly watching the mist rise from the surface of the clear, still lake. One of my favorite memories was sitting at the water's edge in that morning mist with the company of my cherished dog, Cody, staring into the mist, and watching the world come into existence. As the mist lifted, it seemed that the world recreated itself daily. Mary and I often fell asleep in the evenings serenaded by the call of whippoorwills and the honking of the huge bullfrogs that lived along the shore.

We soon discovered that this remote, rural area was very conservative and wondered if a same-sex couple would be accepted in their midst.

Then we met our closest new neighbor, a robust, bold, outspoken, large French Canadian man with a ponytail, hoop earring, and big personality. He embraced us so enthusiastically that we relaxed. However, we were still not sure about being welcomed by many of our neighbors. Most were cordial, some were very friendly, but at the same time seemed to feel uncomfortable around us. We were disheartened to hear one neighbor say that he had moved away from Florida " to get away from the spics and the queers."

Over the next few years, we made many friends. We bought and developed several lakefront properties that were left over after the developers were ready to move on, and I served as president of the POA for its first term. We felt especially honored to get to know and appreciate many of the-long term local residents in this small mountain community as we learned about its history and culture.

The contractor and carpenters who built our house were delightful, kind and respectful. It was not unusual to see one particular carpenter arrive in the morning in his pickup truck with a decomposing chicken in the back. I was a bit put off by that, to say the least. "WHY, Buck?" I asked, "are you driving around with a dead, decaying chicken in your truck?" It became quite natural after he explained to me : "I am a hunter and plan to use it as bait to catch something else. I ride it around in my truck in the warm sunshine to ripen it." He smiled broadly and spat a chew of tobacco. I could tell that he enjoyed telling me the story, so I changed my morning greeting to, "Good morning Buck, I see you brought your lunch again." He would say, "Yessum. You want some, doncha?"

One morning, we arrived at the building site and heard a kitten mewing. A beautiful, tiny and skittish kitten with an orange coat and big blue eyes crept into view. We asked one of the carpenters, "Jim, is this your cat?" "No ma'am, we jus' heard it down at the lake, went down there, and it was trying to get outta the water, almost drowned."

I said, "Oh my, do you know where it might have come from?" Jim replied, "I have not seen an adult female around since we started building. Lots of people, if they don't want a litter of cats, they jus tie 'em up in a sack and throw 'em in a lake or creek to drown 'em. This 'un must of got outta the sack somehow. We jus thought you'ens might want it, so we brung it up here and dried it off and we' been feedin' it."

There was no sign of judgement in Jim's voice about the person who tried to drown the kitten or any comment about them trying to save and feed it for us. It was just a calm, matter-of-fact statement. There was, however, a real tenderness about the way Jim held the kitten and told us about feeding him. We found a great home for the kitten who grew into a really beautiful orange tabby named Lucky.

Were the obstacles we expected in the beginning imaginary? No, not quite. Once, we invited everyone to our home for a summer party. The colorfully illustrated invitation indicated that Sue, whose birthday competed with that of Jesus, would be celebrating in June rather than December. One neighbor left us a phone message saying, "You better git yo' Bible down and study it. Don't ever put anything like this in my mailbox again or I'll report ya!" So I sent a message back, saying, "Does that mean you are not coming?" No, no, I did NOT do that! Of course I did not, but I thought about it.

Breaking ground for the lake house.

    I felt that, over time, the dynamics of the relationships with most people changed as we all became more familiar with each other. It was obvious that some of the people who were friendly did not quite know how to "be" with us, but as time went by, that discomfort seemed to dissipate, with the exception a few very conservative, "Christian" residents.

    As we began to develop relationships with many of the people who lived in the region, the more we appreciated their sense of humor, their kindness and their life styles. We began to discover, and then shed, some of the stereotypical beliefs that we had held about mountain people. When we announced that we were moving, the neighbor who had made the "spics and queers" comment hugged us and invited us to return to visit them in their home. Perhaps they, and others, gave up some of their beliefs about "city folks" and same-sex couples as we all came to know and respect each other as just "people."

THE JUICE IS IN THE JOURNEY | 95

Top: The Roly Hole, lakeside view. Below: Cody, lover boy, lounging on the dock. Right: Mary and Cody exploring the lake by kayak.

21

HOLD MY WINE AND WATCH THIS

Many of us are familiar with having a "senior moment," but did you know that seniors can have "adolescent moments?"

And so it was, on June 3, 2020. I was cleaning the garage of our home in Black Mountain and Mary's bike was in my way, so I decided to roll it outside. That's when it happened: It was a beautiful sunny morning and I thought that a quick bike ride down the driveway and back would feel really good.

In spite of being 86 years old and the fact that I had not been on a bike in years, I hopped on without a problem and headed down the driveway. I picked up speed really quickly on the downhill slope and tried to brake before reaching the street.. OMG! NO BRAKES? The pedals were just spinning backwards as I tried to stop.

Thinking fast, I saw that if I turned right onto the street, I would be flying downhill, so I chose the neighbor's grassy lawn across the street. It sloped downward as well but I thought I could make a quick turn and start back up the incline and slow the bike. TOO LATE! There was a tree in the way, and I was seconds away from hitting a low stone wall— which would surely have sent me flying over the handlebars onto concrete steps. (OF COURSE, I WAS NOT WEARING A HELMET! I was just going to the end of the driveway!) Again, my quick thinking told me to jump off the damn bike—NOW!

As I lay stunned and crumpled on the grass, I noticed that my left knee seemed to be at an odd angle. My next thought was, "Oh shit, the brakes are on the handlebars these days!! Why didn't I think of that?" My yell for help rang through the quiet neighborhood with no response. But, after the 3rd or 4th try, a little girl came out of the house with her mom. Three-year-old Kinley had been playing nearby and ran into her house and said to her mom, "There is a person laying on our lawn and you should come look!"

Kinley, her mom and another neighbor rushed over immediately to help. I gave them my phone and they called 911 then Mary, who was driving to Asheville. A few people gathered while we waited for the ambulance, and Kinley, who had picked little flowers in the yard, brought them over and put them by my face and told me I would be "OK." She attempted to provide more comfort by bringing me her favorite stuffed animal, and she said, "You can keep him until they take you away."

I worried about the horror and stress Mary would no doubt feel when she received this emergency call, and I was also very embarrassed about my brief lapse of memory about the brakes. "What a dumb thing to do!" and " I will never live this down!"

Tracy, a good friend who lived nearby, was alerted by Mary and quickly arrived at the scene. Mary and the ambulance arrived shortly afterward. The paramedics took one look at my leg position and began to cut away my pants—my favorites! They put a brace in place to prevent my leg from moving, and then transported me into the ambulance.

This was obviously not something my body wanted to do, and I kept telling the EMT that I needed to curse REALLY badly! He encouraged me to go for it! But Kinley and a friend of hers, Payton, were watching the show by this time, so I waited until we were inside the ambulance. Once there, I let out a rapid succession of every expletive that I knew just before receiving a welcomed injection that replaced some of my pain with a soft blue haze.

I was soon admitted to the Trauma Unit of Mission Hospital and taken immediately to surgery. Mary was never, ever allowed to enter the hospital because it was during the early days of COVID-19, and was told to wait in the parking lot for messages from the trauma team.

My primary injury was a spiral femoral fracture, which was repaired by placing a titanium rod through my femur from my hip to my knee. The physicians waited until the next day to do more extensive x-rays to make sure there were no other broken bones. The rest of the damage consisted of severe bruising from my rib cage to my foot, which turned out to be more uncomfortable than the fracture. Four days later, I was released from the hospital for rehabilitation at home, with physical therapists coming in twice a week. Expected recovery: 4—6 months!

After two months of rehabilitation, I had improved enough that I ditched the walker and began walking with a cane. The visiting physical therapists were very generous with their compliments regarding my progress. Of course, my secret weapon was my amazing spouse, Mary, who, besides being a first-class retired physical therapist, might have been a boot camp sergeant in another life. She had no problem keeping me on track.

The accident brought Kinley and me together and we became great friends. She and

Payton drew get-well cards for me and brought more flowers when I returned home from the hospital. The sweet relationship continued and, for several months, she visited me in my back yard art studio, which was a helpful distraction from thinking of my unfortunate adolescent moment.

During my rehabilitation, I was gifted with love through the delivery of flowers, cards, e-notes, and even the delivery of delicious meals. Many friends came and sat with me so Mary could feel comfortable leaving for errands or a walk. I had so many wonderful surprises!

I also never knew that I had so many friends and family members who are real smart-asses and found the details of my accident quite entertaining. Even a physician at Mission Hospital told me I was the star patient of the week because, every day on rounds, a resident or physician would report on me, reading the chart as follows: "86-year-old white female jumps from speeding bike and fractures femur and severely bruises entire body... REALLY?"

Fortunately, I thrive on this kind of love and attention and, although I do not want to pick favorites, I will confess that the title of this piece—"Hold My Wine and Watch This"—was printed on a coffee mug with a bike symbol that was a gift from a young family member. Ha!!

Left: Kinley, my across-the-street neighbor, with a personalized get well card and, above, the bike with no brakes... I thought.

22

LEAKING TIME

Around the time I turned 80, I developed a curiosity and preoccupation about the passage of time and the finality of life. I am a laboratory on aging, where I observe and document the changes occurring in my mind, body and emotions.

One of the more fascinating observations seems to be the tendency to blame every ache and pain or change in appearance on age. Another is navigating the subtle conflicts between cultural assumptions about how we are supposed to act as elders, as opposed to how we have always acted. Often there is an awkward dance around those expectations.

There are also denial tricks the mind can play: When I am attempting to focus on serious things to consider, like health issues, leaving loved ones, and estate planning—so as to not to leave a mess for others to clean up—all I can think of is silly things, like, "I hope I can keep my teeth."

I have also been hoping, with my history of procrastination and the tendency to become more creative as a deadline approaches, that I would actually complete some of the many projects that have been in progress, or ones that I have been contemplating for years. This memoir could be first on the list. There are several beautiful stones in my studio gathering dust that beg to be carved and canvases that want to be painted. This is just the short list of things I'd like to complete.

My most dreaded concern is not as much about being dead, but how I arrive there. The thought of possibly losing my mind, or being in a hospital or nursing home frightens me more than dying. And I ask myself: "so, how would I prefer to leave this life?"

As I detailed in Chapter 19, my Mom set the bar pretty high for an ideal way to die. Enjoying a long and active life for 85 years, she was sick for only a week. Totally alert and choosing not to have life-extending procedures that would leave her an invalid, she slipped into a coma for a few hours and died surrounded by her family. I would consider myself very fortunate to have a similar kind of death.

Then there is the question of what to do with my remains. Would I prefer to have a funeral or memorial service, and what would it be like? Oddly, this has been the most entertaining aspect to contemplate. After the easy decisions of being cremated and having my loved ones scatter my ashes in some favorite spot in these beautiful mountains, the possibilities expand. My favorite fantasy is this:

Several of my family members and closest friends gather in a private location for a catered, gourmet dinner with fine wine and music, at my expense, of course! During dinner, they would suddenly hear my voice greeting them and sharing some funny anecdotes about the outer realms and the kinds of things that might be expected of them before they can enter "the pearly gates." Sometimes I also consider including a brief video of me doing a comic dance routine to a Buddy Holly tune or some other familiar music as the video fades into vapor.

Maybe my friends and family would be mortified, but planning it makes me smile!

EPILOGUE
Remembering Oneness

Life is a circle and I am back at the beginning... remembering.

This old one can no longer walk in the warm, soft, freshly plowed earth.

My father and Pete can no longer prepare the rich brown earth for a new crop.

But I can still hear the sounds of the traces, the soft "gees" and "haws" and feel the warmth of the sun.

I can sense the sweet warm earth, the man and animal smells as they blend with some far away cadence beyond this world.

THE END

GRATITUDE

My writing coach, Victoria Fann, provided the fuel for writing about this journey. Her wisdom and encouragement kept me on-track during her classes on creative writing, and gave me the courage to share my story. She has been my guide throughout this process.

I offer over-the-top gratitude to Odette Colón for the many hours, days and weeks of time she generously provided for her artistic design, creative illustrations and thoughtful layout of this memoir. Her recommendations, expertise and gentle guidance were from her heart… and filled mine.

A huge THANK YOU to my editor, Mike Czeczot. Without his advice, this memoir wouldn't have a single comma! His humor and critical attention have been invaluable.

I'm forever indebted to my beta readers, who generously offered their time, ongoing encouragement, suggestions and support while I was writing this memoir: Jane Fishman, Cindi Johnson, Nancy Pope, Jackie Tatelman, Jennifer Carter, and Janet Brumfield. Their honest feedback was so very helpful, and assisted my navigation and reflection about this life's journey. Many thanks, Y'all!

Finally, my thanks to a most helpful writing group. We met together regularly for a year or more, sharing our efforts, giving each other feedback and encouragement. Priceless, my friends!

IN MEMORIAM
Nancy Hull Cramer
1942—2023

Nan Cramer and I were close friends and business partners since the 1960s. Her humor and deep understanding of the human condition was the hallmark of P&H's work. Nan was also an intergral part of my personal success.